April 2015

To

With Best Wishes

Nicky

Captain ALAC

GULLANE LADIES' GOLF CLUB

THE FIRST ONE HUNDRED YEARS

1904-2004

Compiled with help from members and others by

Shona Low
Connie Lugton
Kay McLean Ross
Margaret Sneddon
Ethel Jack

“Gullane Ladies’ Golf Club
The First One Hundred Years
1904-2004”

First published in Great Britain in 2003 by

Shona Low
Thornfield
2 Erskine Loan
Gullane
EH31 2EH

ISBN: 0-9539268-1-8

Book design: Andrew Burns gave advice on the layout of the book. Shona Low planned the detail design. Peter Fox designed the cover.

Photographs: The photographs used are either the property of Gullane Ladies’ Golf Club or of the subject except as stated below the photograph. Joyce Murdoch produced all the photographs on disk either from existing material or by taking a new photograph.

Printed by: David Macdonald Limited
25 Rodney Street
Edinburgh
EH7 4EL

CONTENTS

Judith Cuthbertson

Captain 2003 - 2004

FOREWORD

It is a privilege to be asked to write a foreword to the book of the history of our Club. My husband, Evan, was Captain of Gullane Golf Club during their Centenary in 1982 and I am honoured to be Captain of Gullane Ladies for our Centenary. I have been a member for nearly 40 years and was secretary for five of them. I have seen many changes as the Club moved through the twentieth and into the twenty-first centuries.

We are all fiercely proud of our independence and long history. The reader will see that we have, and have had, many talented and well-known golfers in our membership. Engineered by my mother-in-law, Shelagh, I was proposed for membership by Charlotte Beddows, no less, and when I became a member I discovered with awe who she was. I prayed that she would not ask me to play with her, as at that time I had a handicap of 36*.

Over the years we have enjoyed a very good relationship with the men of Gullane Golf Club, both on the golf course and in the Clubhouse. May this continue for the next one hundred years.

There was a wealth of information in the past records in the cupboard in the changing rooms - minutes of meetings, treasurers' records, letters from members, photographs, etc. The researchers and writers of this book have found their job fascinating. Many members have contributed their own memories.

This book will become an essential reference book for Club members and others. I have already been dipping into it for information.

Judith Cuthbertson

Photograph by Joyce Murdoch

The Book Committee

Shona Low, Kay McLean Ross, Margaret Sneddon, Ethel Jack

PREFACE

When the Captain, Margaret Sneddon, asked me if I would look into producing a book of the history of Gullane Ladies' Golf Club in April 2001 for the Centenary of the Club in 2004, I had no idea of the fascinating task ahead.

Together with Margaret herself, Kay McLean Ross and Connie Lugton, all members with a great love of and interest in the Club, we set out to find out what had happened in the past. Connie had a fund of knowledge of people and events that had happened in Gullane and in the golfing world. When she very sadly died in January 2003 she left an enormous gap in our group as she had been a unique source of information relating to the village, the Club and Scottish golf. Ethel Jack, with an invaluable experience in Scottish golf and a long time member of the Club, stepped very ably into her shoes.

After we realised that we would have to compile the book ourselves we decided to concentrate on the people who have made GLGC the Club it is today. Our task was made easier by the detailed minutes that had been kept -Margaret and I have been through them so often we feel we have lived through all the meetings!

Kay volunteered for the tedious task of scouring past newspapers in the History Library at Haddington and she would like to thank the staff there who gave her so much help. Margaret chased up our Life Honorary members and past Captains for information. We appealed to the members to search their memories, attics and photograph albums for interesting anecdotes and pictures. Many thanks indeed to all of you who helped in this way. We are indebted to Joyce Murdoch for the excellent job she did in putting all our photographs and information onto disc and also in taking many photos at the Club.

In producing this book, we have all ended up with enormous respect for our forebears and immense pride in the achievements of the Club over its first one hundred years. We hope that it will be enjoyed by all who are interested, not only in GLGC but also in many of the best Scottish lady golfers of the 20th Century.

Shona Low

The British Ladies' Championship at Gullane, 1897

THE BEGINNING

On 1st December 1904, fourteen ladies gathered in Dowell's rooms, Edinburgh, for the first meeting of Gullane Ladies' Golf Club. These fourteen together with another thirty three ladies were the first members of the Club (Appendix 1). They would be very proud to see Gullane Ladies' Golf Club today—one of the largest and most prestigious Ladies' Clubs in Britain.

The earliest reference to ladies playing golf at Gullane is given by John Kerr, when, writing about a tournament for the men on August 20, 1892, he mentions that

" The day previous saw a successful tournament, also over Gullane, in which 27 ladies took part, the round consisting of 12 holes. Miss L.J. Lugton, a local player, won the first prize with an excellent 64."

The Golf Book of East Lothian, John Kerr. P165

Ladies' golf in Gullane received a huge boost in 1897 when the British Ladies' Championship was held there. It was the third time that the Championship had been held and the first time in Scotland.

" The Scottish Ladies were delighted to find they were not at all outclassed and indeed the Championship was won by Miss E.C. Orr from North Berwick defeating her sister in the final. This competition was not simply a success; it marked a new era in golf. ...there were many who vowed they would not go near Gullane, because they had the impression that the game of the ladies was not worth seeing. All this has been dispelled...".

East Lothian Courier, 1897

Perhaps the Courier was a little optimistic but, from this time on, ladies took part in increasing numbers of club competitions. As this anecdote shows, reported in 1951 after the British Girl's Championship was held at Gullane, people were as interested in the progress of amateur events as they are in professional events nowadays.

" As a semi final match in the Championship was coming down the seventeenth fairway a bus came along the road. The conductor did not hesitate but rang the bell, stopped the bus and got out along with several passengers.

They watched the hole played out and the passengers clambered back. The conductor was too engrossed in watching the drive from the tee to get aboard. It was only after the bus started he realised the position and had to put in a McDonald–Bailey–like sprint to catch up with his vehicle which was bowling along merrily. In the end some of the passengers noticed his predicament, the bus stopped once more and the red faced servant of the State returned to his normal station"

Golf Illustrated Magazine, 1951

In September 1904 Mr Richard Watson, a member of Gullane Golf Club and Captain in 1906, arranged an open hole–and–handicap tournament in ladies singles which took place over Gullane Old Course. This proved such a success that in November 1904 the Courier reported the proposal to form a club to be called Gullane Ladies' Golf Club. Mr Richard Watson was the driving force behind this proposal.

Mr Richard Watson

Photo courtesy of Gullane Golf Club

"The announcement that the initial stages towards the formation of the club have been carried through by Mr Watson is tantamount to saying that success is already assured."

East Lothian Courier, November 1904

Mr and Mrs Watson and Miss Dowell promised to make the arrangements for the constitution of the Club and proposed the inaugural meeting for the 1st December 1904 in Dowell's Rooms in Edinburgh.

Formation of the Club

" It was decided to form a club to be called Gullane Ladies' Golf Club, the first members of which would consist of the fourteen Ladies present, along with another thirty three Ladies who had intimated their intention of joining the Club on its formation"

Minutes GLGC 1904

The first meeting was constituted with Mr Richard Watson acting as Chairman. The constitution was decided and a Committee of seven members was elected. All the members elected to serve on the Committee had houses in the village. Mrs Watson (Dunville, now The Gables) was elected Honorary Secretary and Treasurer. Other members of this first committee were Miss Dowell (Dilston), Mrs Alloway (Sunnybank), Mrs George Cotton (The Ferns now Mayfield), Miss Mabel Law (Lammerview Terrace) , Mrs Caesar (The Manse), the wife of the minister and Miss L. Lugton (Westbourne), the winner of the first reported ladies' competition at Gullane in 1892. Lady Spearman (Craigour) was elected the first President of the Club.

It was considered important to have a Clubhouse for the ladies to use which was separate from Gullane Golf Club to emphasise that a separate Club was being formed. A place to leave golfing jackets was also necessary as they were an important part of ladies' golfing apparel. In 1897 the Courier was rather smugly enjoying the success of the Scottish ladies in the Championship.

" Comparing North with South, it was noticeable that English ladies, far more than those from Scotland, went in for red jackets and showy garments, and indeed pursued the gutta in a more masculine fashion all round.

No red–jacketed player was, however, in the semi–final, so that the orthodox garment can have in itself no saving virtue. Simplicity itself characterised the dress of the two sister finalists, and their quiet, modest, unassuming manner won for them both the hearts of all who witnessed their play"
East Lothian Courier 1897

The initial objectives of the club, as decided at the first meeting, were

1. To hold two or more competitions in the year.
2. To arrange matches with other ladies' golf clubs.
3. To provide some kind of clubhouse or shelter where golf clubs, jackets and other belongings could be left.

Because of the leases of the Old and New courses to Gullane Golf Club the ladies could not have special rights to play on them so that they would have to take daily, monthly or yearly tickets as was usual. However the Ladies' Course was available free of charge.

GLGC Clubhouse from1911-1922

The Old Post Office and Gullane Reading Room-now the Golf Museum with Miss Isabella Scott, postmistress, great great aunt of Mrs Margaret Sneddon, Captain, 2001-02

Photograph courtesy of the Gullane & Dirleton History Society

THE CLUBHOUSE

From the beginning of GLGC provision of their own clubhouse was a major objective of the Club. It was one of the resolutions of the first Committee meeting in December 1904.

The Committee proposed to rent a room from Mr George Leishman at Marionville at a rental of £6 per annum for the initial membership and an increase of £1 for each 10 additional members. This proposal subsequently fell through as Mr Leishman let the entire house for a considerable portion of the season. Instead the members rented a large shed in Saltcoats Road belonging to Alex Aitken, the Gullane clubmaker. The terms of the agreement were agreed on 10th February 1905 with a rent of £5 per year and a small additional piece of ground available if required in the future. Mr H.K. Wilson, builder, was instructed to install lavatory accommodation at a cost of £12: 15/-. This Clubhouse served the club well until membership started to increase in 1911 and more space was required.

In 1911 GLGC sublet the Gullane Reading Clubroom attached to the old Post Office from Rev. R. Howie. This space is now occupied by Archie Baird's

Shepherd's Cottage.
The Clubhouse from 1922-1928

Golf Museum beside the Professional's Golf shop. The rental was still £5 per annum and Mr Wilson removed the lavatory fittings from Saltcoats Road and installed them in the new Clubhouse. During the First World War there was little golfing activity but afterwards the increasing number of members demanded improved clubhouse premises.

In 1920 GLGC entered into negotiations with Mr Curr, Factor of the Dirleton Estate owned by Colonel Hamilton Grant. Mr Curr offered to grant the feu of the house and garden at the West End of Gullane - known by the name of Shepherd's Cottage - at the annual feu duty of £10. The Ladies conducted extensive negotiations on the terms of the Feu Charter through Mrs Wallace Williamson, the Honorary Secretary at the time, and their lawyer Mr Hugh Lennox. It was not enough that the building was made wind and waterproof, Mr Curr demanded that it be made good to the value of £300. As the property at that time was worth £100 at the most he was, in effect, demanding that the ladies spend £200 on improving the building. The ladies could not afford this and further negotiations took place.

Eventually a compromise was reached. The Feu Charter was finally granted in May 1922 on condition that the building was improved to the value of £300 in five years. The Ladies agreed to this. There were two other terms which are of interest: the ground at the back could be used as a tennis court (this never happened) and, crucially, the Ladies had the power to take down and rebuild the house.

The Captain and Secretary were given powers to buy small necessities for the Clubhouse:

"Curtains and table covers, tin deed box, table, face towels, match boxes, cork carpet for stair, 2 butter and 2 jam dishes, 1 doz. stainless knives, large ink pot, an address stamp, 3 lavatory towels, shelf paper, waste paper basket, blotter, 1 calendar. Also to keep soap and matches etc in store."

GLGC Minutes 1922

This Clubhouse was well used. In 1922 it was decided that

"in future no dogs be allowed in the Clubhouse and no smoking in the main clubroom be permitted between the hours of 2 and 5p.m. to allow members to start their tea before the room was filled with smoke. It was also decided that a gas radiator should be put in the other upstairs room so that anyone wishing to play Bridge should stay in that room."

GLGC Minutes 1922

The issue of where members played bridge has occupied much thought in committees over the years!

Altogether the renovating of the Clubhouse cost £92:10/3. In 1923 a compulsory levy of £1 was imposed on all members to raise funds for the Clubhouse improvements. This brought in £160. However it does not seem that the Clubhouse was very luxurious as there was much concern for the comfort of visitors to the

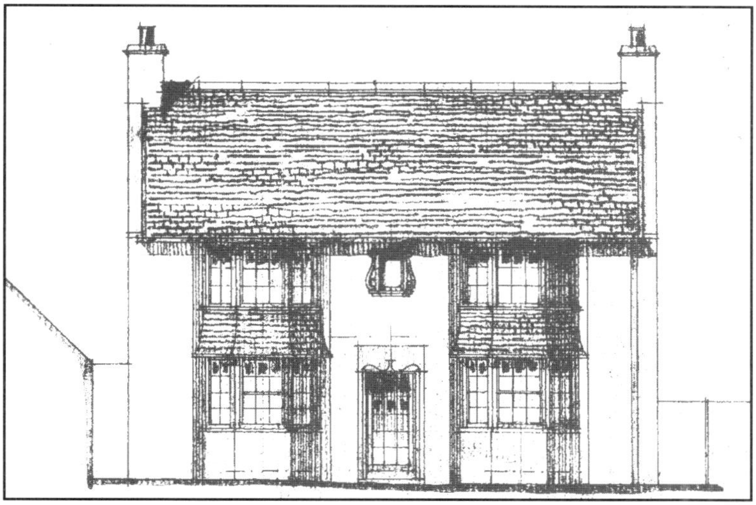

Sir Robert Lorimer's plans for the new Clubhouse in 1926

Scottish Ladies' Golf Championship in 1925. The Committee decided that comfortable chairs were to be brought downstairs to the kitchen where tea, coffee, Bovril, biscuits etc would be supplied for all players.

According to the agreement in the Feu Charter, the Clubhouse had to be made good to the value of £300 by November 1926. The Ladies decided that it would make more economic sense to knock down Shepherd's Cottage and rebuild a new Clubhouse on the site. Colonel Hamilton Grant agreed to this subject to his approval of plans. Accordingly they asked Sir Robert Lorimer, the eminent architect, to draw up plans. The cost would be approximately £1450. The proposed Clubroom sounds most attractive. It was to extend the whole length of the proposed building, lined with three-ply boarding with cover mouldings over the joints, and have a coved plaster ceiling with a brick fireplace at each end. Colonel Grant certainly approved, writing that the elevation presented a very attractive appearance.

The Ladies held an Extraordinary General Meeting in 1926 and it was decided to go ahead with the Lorimer plan. The money for the rebuild was to be raised by donations, a Sale of Work and the balance by debentures.

Shepherd's Cottage with adjoining cottages. These were all demolished to make room for the new Clubhouse

Copy of newspaper cutting from album owned by Mr Alistair McIntosh

"Bazaar at Gullane—Under the auspices of the Gullane Ladies' Golf Club, a bazaar was yesterday held, by courtesy of Mr & Mrs A.W. Robertson Durham, in the grounds of The Warren at Gullane. The bazaar was in aid of the building fund of the club—a new clubhouse being contemplated. ..The sale realised about £204."

East Lothian Courier. Sept 1927

Two significant developments then took place. The Ladies were given the opportunity to buy the cottage adjoining their Clubhouse which was let to a man called MacLeod. He had been promised one of the County Council houses at Orr's Nursery Gardens and hence the owners wished to dispose of this cottage. Secondly, Gullane Golf Club decided that they required a new Clubhouse. The site of the Ladies' Clubhouse being considered the best place for a new building, negotiations were set in place for the two Clubs to agree on the terms for developing a joint Clubhouse.

Sir Robert Lorimer's plans were shelved and GGC undertook to build a new joint Clubhouse using Mr N. B. Taylor as architect. The plans were discussed at the AGM of Gullane Golf Club in September 1927.

" The situation proposed for the new building is the site of the present clubhouse of Gullane Ladies' Golf Club. The ladies' clubhouse was regarded only as of a temporary nature, being inadequate for the requirements of that club, which is in a flourishing state, and the new scheme of erection on the ladies' site provides for the accommodation - although not an amalgamation - of both the Gullane Club and Gullane Ladies' Club within the same clubhouse, each, however, retaining its separate identity."
East Lothian Courier. September 1927

The negotiations did not get off to a very good start. In October 1927, the Ladies and their lawyer, Hugh Lennox, were not pleased to hear from Colonel Grant's agents, Dundas and Wilson, that arrangements had been made with Gullane Golf Club which involved reconveyancing to the Superior a portion of the site feued to the Ladies' Golf Club. Mr Lennox wrote back to Dundas and Wilson, in a very restrained manner,

"details had not yet been submitted to the Ladies and we were not aware of the proposal that part of the Ladies' site should be resumed by the Superior".
Letter from Hugh Lennox to Dundas and Wilson. 1927

He was not quite so restrained when he reported on this to the Ladies:

"I did not want to show any feeling in our letter but

we might easily have commented on the fact that apparently without consulting the Ladies' Club arrangements had been made for dispensing of part of their property"!

Letter from Hugh Lennox to Miss Robertson Durham. 1927

Needless to say Mr Lennox, the Secretary Miss Robertson Durham (who became Mrs Ian Bowhill) and the Captain, her aunt, Mrs Dryborough were determined that any agreement should be as watertight as possible to protect the interests of the current and future members. Eventually agreement was reached in April 1928. The terms are discussed in a later section but, so far, they have proved extremely sound in protecting the interests of GLGC.

The Ladies were not asked for any money to help with the building of the Clubhouse although the level of subscription became part of the agreement between the clubs. While the building was going on GLGC was offered the use of a hut in the grounds of Glencairn, the house owned by Mrs A. W. Robertson Durham. The Ladies' accommodation in the new Clubhouse was to consist of a common dining room, a common lounge, private club room, dressing room and lockers.

"A start has been made with the clearing of the site for the new clubhouse of the Gullane Golf Club. The red tiled cottages at No.1 teeing box are being pulled down, and the new clubhouse will be erected on the site."

East Lothian Courier. July 1928

On pulling down the Ladies' old Clubhouse, a coping stone was found which was built into the new Clubhouse above the entrance to the Ladies' locker room. The inscription on the coping stone, which is still there, is:

17 WC ♥ MD 28

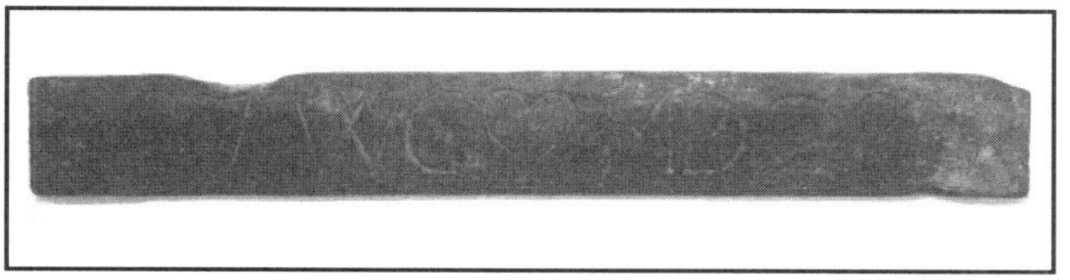

Coping stone in Shepherd's Cottage; now above the entrance to the Ladies' Locker room.

Photograph by Joyce Murdoch

The Ladies had complete autonomy in furnishing their part of the new Clubhouse at a sum not exceeding £430. Mrs Dorothy Rome, Captain at the time, worked extremely hard, together with her Committee, to provide a suitable clubhouse for GLGC members. Estimates and plans were submitted from Heals, Peter Jones, Weston Miller, Wylie and Lochhead and Jenners. Heals and Jenners made it to the final list with Jenners laying out a room of furniture for the Committee to see. However the estimate from Heals of London was accepted and they produced tables and chairs still admired and in use today. In November 1929 a further £100 was approved by the members for the Committee to spend on additional furnishings.

This new, and current, Clubhouse was opened by Mrs Rome, on December 21st 1930. From that time to today the Ladies have been settled in their part of the Clubhouse.

The preoccupations of the Committees in the early 30s were mainly about

Ladies' lounge with the original Heal's furniture

photograph by Joyce Murdoch

The current Clubhouse for GLGC and GGC

Photograbh by Joyce Murdoch

where bridge was to be played and what catering was to be provided. Some members even brought their own lunch or tea but this was not acceptable and the offending members were told they could not eat their own food in the Clubhouse! There was a complaint that the lemons in drinks were not cut thin enough and ice was requested all the year round.

During the Second World War years the Clubhouse was used for many things other than for golf matters. The WVS was granted the use of the Clubroom to make hospital dressings etc. The Red Cross Work Party met in the Clubroom on two afternoons a week and in return the British Red Cross sent a load of logs for use during the winter. A Bridge Party was held to raise funds for the Golfers' Spitfire Fund. As a reward for the best contribution to the fund GLGC were asked to choose their prize. They chose the propeller from a downed German bomber. Unfortunately no one seems to know what happened to this propeller. A small plaque on the side of the fireplace in the Ladies' lounge is the only evidence of this award.

After the War things reverted to normal slowly. Since then one of the main issues has been decorating and modifying the lounge, locker room and cloakroom. This is an ongoing aspect as the needs of different times have to be taken into account. Currently the lockers, built for the Ladies' bags of the 30s, are too small for the more elaborate bags and sets of clubs of the 21st century. Catering in the

Clubhouse has been a frequent problem. The caterers have to work for both GGC and GLGC and it seems that often the two clubs have wanted different things. However Miss Christian Thin recalls that

"In the 40s my parents and myself had rounds of golf followed by scrumptious home baked teas upstairs in the mixed lounge. I do remember it was very welcoming with comfortable sofas and chairs"

Miss Christian Thin, member

Over the years many changes have taken place inside the Clubhouse to try and accommodate the needs of a greater number of members. The Ladies have contributed considerably to these developments as well as to other aspects of the running of the Club. They paid for the installation of additional lockers in 1936. During the Second World War GLGC paid the wages of one maid (£70 for the year). This was stopped in 1945. In the early fifties GGC found that they had

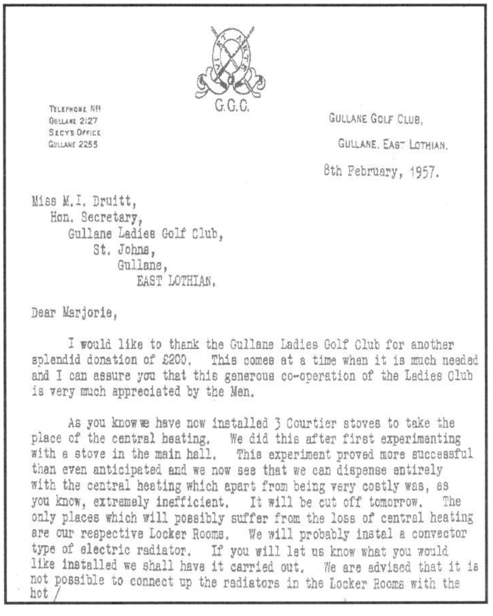

G.G.C.

TELEPHONE Nº
GULLANE 2127
SECY'S OFFICE
GULLANE 2255

GULLANE GOLF CLUB,
GULLANE, EAST LOTHIAN.

8th February, 1957.

Miss M.I. Druitt,
Hon. Secretary,
Gullane Ladies Golf Club,
St. Johns,
Gullane,
EAST LOTHIAN.

Dear Marjorie,

I would like to thank the Gullane Ladies Golf Club for another splendid donation of £200. This comes at a time when it is much needed and I can assure you that this generous co-operation of the Ladies Club is very much appreciated by the Men.

As you know we have now installed 3 Courtier stoves to take the place of the central heating. We did this after first experimenting with a stove in the main hall. This experiment proved more successful than even anticipated and we now see that we can dispense entirely with the central heating which apart from being very costly was, as you know, extremely inefficient. It will be cut off tomorrow. The only places which will possibly suffer from the loss of central heating are our respective Locker Rooms. We will probably instal a convector type of electric radiator. If you will let us know what you would like installed we shall have it carried out. We are advised that it is not possible to connect up the radiators in the Locker Rooms with the hot /

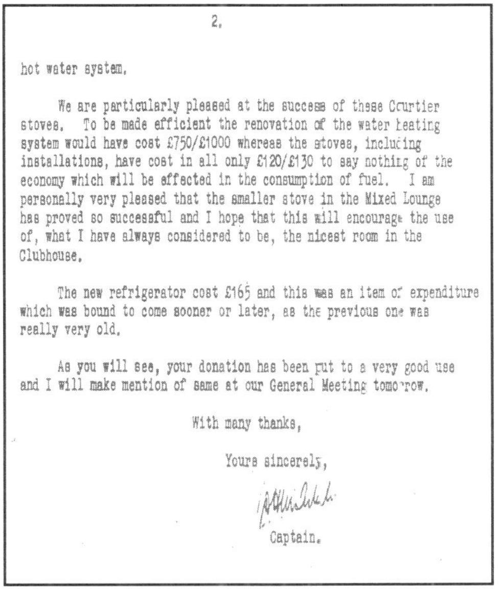

2.

hot water system.

We are particularly pleased at the success of these Courtier stoves. To be made efficient the renovation of the water heating system would have cost £750/£1000 whereas the stoves, including installations, have cost in all only £120/£130 to say nothing of the economy which will be effected in the consumption of fuel. I am personally very pleased that the smaller stove in the Mixed Lounge has proved so successful and I hope that this will encourage the use of, what I have always considered to be, the nicest room in the Clubhouse.

The new refrigerator cost £165 and this was an item of expenditure which was bound to come sooner or later, as the previous one was really very old.

As you will see, your donation has been put to a very good use and I will make mention of same at our General Meeting tomorrow.

With many thanks,

Yours sincerely,

Captain.

Letter of appreciation from GGC

financial problems and so, although it was not part of the agreement made with the men, the Ladies contributed towards the upkeep of the Clubhouse: they paid for the redecoration of their lounge and cloakroom, gave a contribution to the refurbishment of the mixed lounge, provided an additional £200 to GGC, three stoves and a new refrigerator and in 1960 paid for new curtains in the Card Room (£34: 17/6).

In 1964 the Ladies' locker room was enlarged and the Ladies were asked if they could contribute £3000 towards the cost. The money was raised by three sources: a levy from the members over 3 years; £800 from Club funds and a donation of £500 from Dr Leeds. This enabled the extension to go ahead. Since then the Ladies have paid for the refurbishment of the Ladies' Lounge and the Locker Room although always trying to retain the style and period of the rooms.

In 1997 the advent of the computer could not be ignored. A new handicapping system was introduced by the LGU which, for a club the size of GLGC, required the use of a computer. An office was made out of the drying room and new drying cupboards installed. The office is now seen as indispensable and holds the records of the Club along with the computer and its peripherals.

As the number of visitors to Gullane increased the requirement for adequate changing facilities for both men and women increased. A separate Visitors' Centre was built in 1993 for the use of the many players visiting the Club. This has led to a review of the use of the joint Clubhouse. In January 2001 a survey of all members was organised by Gullane Golf Club regarding the provision of the Club's catering services. The results indicated a groundswell of opinion in favour of making these services more informal and flexible. A significant number of members wished to see this achieved as part of a comprehensive redevelopment of the Clubhouse. However after extensive further consultation the two Clubs decided to look at the future relationship between the Clubs before final decisions were made. Exploratory meetings with representatives from both Clubs are considering "The Way Forward". No doubt this dilemma will be resolved in the next century of GLGC.

A Committee Meeting!

Sketch by Mrs. Rosemary Forbes

MANAGEMENT OF THE CLUB

In 1904 a Committee was appointed to run the affairs of GLGC. The President was Lady Spearman, the Secretary and Treasurer was Mrs Watson and there were six other members as detailed in the first chapter. There was not a Captain as such but the Senior member of the Committee, elected annually, presided over the AGM. When Lady Spearman died in 1909 the Committee decided that a Captain should be elected.

Captains

The Club minutes for October 1909 suggests that Miss L. Lugton was to be the first Captain elected for 1910. There must have been some problem which has not been recorded as Mrs Alloway, who was the Senior member of the Committee continued in her role of presiding over the AGM and Miss Lugton did not become Captain until 1912. At the AGM of October 1910 it was agreed that the Senior Member of Committee should, in future, be elected as the Captain of the Club.

Mrs George Cotton, as Senior Member of Committee, became the first formally elected Captain in 1911.

This method of electing the Captain annually continued until 1933. The only break was during the First World War when it was decided that the Captain and Committee should remain unchanged for the duration of the War. However the Captain in 1916, Miss E.A.Wise, only continued in office until January 1918 when she resigned her membership. Mrs Nicholson was elected Captain in her place and remained Captain for 1919.

In November 1932 the members at the AGM agreed to alter the method of electing the Captain. The Captain was to be elected at the AGM, from nominations, and to hold office for two years. The following year three nominations were received: Miss Millicent Couper, Lady Handyside and Mrs R.H. Wallace Williamson. Mrs Wallace Williamson was appointed Captain. This is the only time in the history of the Club that the position of Captain has been contested. Subsequently the Committee proposed a member for Captain who was then seconded and elected at the AGM.

In 1964 Miss May Lennox, one of the original members of the Club and a past Captain, presented a silver board on which the names of all Captains of GLGC were to be inscribed. The list of Captains is given in Appendix 2.

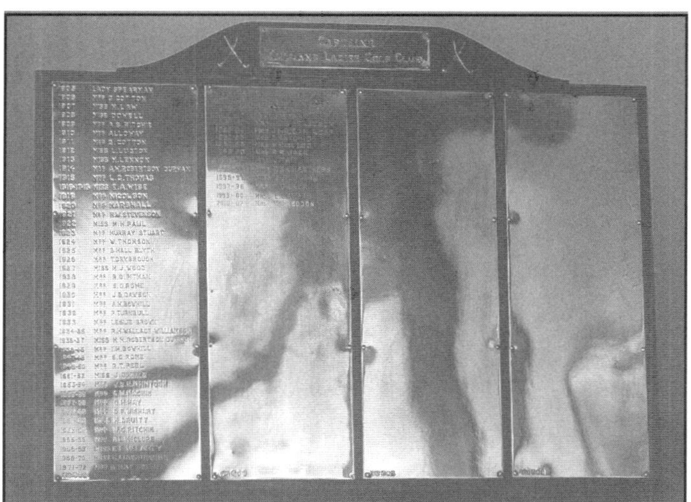

The Captains' Board Presented by Miss May Lennox in 1964

Photograph by Joyce Murdoch

Vice Captains

As the Club expanded and the number of members increased, the commitment required from the Captain increased as well. In 1965 the then Captain, Mrs McClure, proposed that a Vice Captain be elected to the Committee. There were two main reasons for this: firstly, as this person would normally be the next Captain, she would know more about the current business of the Committee when she took office by being on the Committee in advance; secondly to give support to the Captain in her duties.

This was approved at the AGM. Since then the Committee propose a Vice Captain who has to be seconded and elected at the AGM. Both Captain and Vice Captain are eligible for re–election for a second year. In 1975 it was decided that the Vice Captain should act as Match Secretary as well as supporting the Captain in her duties.

Honorary Secretaries

This is one of the most important posts in ensuring the efficient running of the Club. The list of Honorary Secretaries is given in Appendix 3. Miss Marjorie Druitt was the longest serving Secretary as she was in post for thirty years from 1930 to 1960 and then for another two years from 1963 -65. She was also Honorary Treasurer more or less at the same time so must have had a huge influence on the running of the Club.

The job of Secretary has had its lighter moments. Anne Sime recalled some of the incidents during her term of office.

"Two ladies came into the Clubhouse on a Medal Day and informed me that neither were returning their score. It transpired that it was not because they had played badly but because having begun their round quite correctly on No.3 course they had inadvertently finished on No. 2 course. I may say neither were new members—

one had been a member for 15 years!

Then there was the case of the two ladies who were seen walking back to the tee—not because they had lost their balls but because they had been so busy talking they had forgotten to drive!

In one of our Summer Meetings a member came in with an excellent score of 4 below her handicap. After she had signed and posted her card in the Medal Box she informed me that at the 2nd hole she had suffered an unplayable lie in the rough. As dropping her ball 2 club lengths hadn't enabled her to be free of the rough she had taken it out 3 club lengths. She hoped this was all right!"

Anne Sime, Hon. Secretary 1982 -89

Honorary Treasurers

Although initially Mrs Watson was both Honorary Secretary and Treasurer when the Club started, she gave up the post of treasurer in 1911 when the Club made a financial agreement with Gullane Golf Club. Her husband then became Honorary Treasurer and he was followed by another man, Mr Marshall. Since 1923 the Treasurer has been a member of Gullane Ladies' Golf Club. The list of Honorary Treasurers is given in Appendix 3.

Handicap Secretary

The LGU has been in charge of the Handicapping system since it was introduced. To ensure that the system worked properly a Handicap Manager was appointed by the LGU to each affiliated club to control the handicapping of its members. This person was not necessarily a member of the clubs for which she was responsible.

The first Handicap Manager, Mrs Wallace Williamson, was a member but the next two were not. They were made Honorary Members while they acted as Gullane Ladies' Golf Club Handicap Manager. In 1965 the LGU decreed that each club should appoint their own Handicap Secretary from among their membership. At

GLGC this person then became an ex officio member of Committee. The list is given in Appendix 3.

When a new, more complex handicapping system was introduced in 1997, the LGU recommended that each club appoint a Handicap Committee. The Handicap Committee at GLGC comprises four members with the Handicap Secretary representing the Handicap Committee on the main Committee.

Membership Secretary

As the number of members increased and as the waiting list lengthened so the work of keeping track of all members and candidates increased. When the current structure of the waiting list was introduced in 1997 the task became even more complex. It was decided that a specific Membership Secretary should be appointed who would also be an ex officio member of Committee. Until then the Secretary had kept all pertinent records. Connie Lugton became the first Membership Secretary from 1997-2002. Gillian Kirkwood is the current Membership Secretary.

Members of GLGC in 2003

THE MEMBERS

The Early Years
1905– 1911

The Club prospered quickly and by May 1905 fifty members had been enrolled.

One of the major benefits of the Club was in being able to purchase railway tickets between Edinburgh and Gullane at a significant discount. This presented a considerable incentive to joining the Club as most of the members were based in Edinburgh and although they usually had other accommodation in Gullane the train was the best means of transport. This option became less of an advantage as the use of cars increased until in 1925 the Treasurer reported that only 18 tickets had been used. It was decided that GLGC should discontinue buying their own railway tickets and instead use the men's tickets.

Membership of GLGC did not carry any playing rights - all GLGC members had to take daily, weekly or monthly tickets as did everyone else who was not a member of GGC. In spite of the initial benefit of the railway tickets, the Club began to stagnate slightly and the membership which reached 65 in 1907 began to fall back and in 1909 had decreased back to 59 members. In 1910 Miss Lugton and Miss Dowell supported by Mrs Watson proposed a new agreement to be arranged with GGC and a new structure for the Club. It was suggested that this new agreement, which would grant playing rights to members of GLGC, would provide tangible benefits to members and thus attract new members.

1911 Agreement with GGC

After negotiation an agreement was reached with Gullane Golf Club from the 1st March 1911 whereby GLGC paid a sum, 22/6, to GGC for each member of the Club, except for families of Feuars and Proprietors in Gullane who had the right previous to 1905 to play free of charge. In return the members had the right to play on Gullane Nos. 2 and 3 with special rates for permits to play on No. 1. There was the additional benefit that two competitions could be played on No. 1 free of additional charge each year.

To accommodate these changes the Ladies proposed that the present Club was reconstituted to include two classes of members – those paying fees for Nos. 1, 2 and 3 and those only paying fees for Nos. 2 and 3. This was agreed.

1912–1930

The effect of the advantageous agreement with GGC was that membership of GLGC increased very quickly rising to 129 by 1914. The First World War was, naturally, a time of retrenchment of the club with membership dropping back to 81 and little activity. However in 1920 competitions restarted and by 1922 membership was up to 138.

The membership at this time still comprised mainly Edinburgh ladies.

"An application for membership by Miss M. Smith, Golf Hotel, Gullane was considered. As the feeling of the committee was against admitting village girls to the Club, it was decided to ask Miss Smith's proposer and seconder to explain this to Miss Smith and ask her to withdraw the application".

Minutes GLGC October 1920

Known affectionately as Mumsie Smith, Miss Smith, not unexpectedly, reacted to this rebuff by starting up a new golf club restricted to ladies living in Gullane; Dirleton Castle Ladies' Golf Club. This prejudice against "village girls" has not lasted, fortunately. Mumsie Smith's daughter, Mrs Catherine Tait, became Captain of GLGC in 1991.

GLGC members spectating at the Scottish Ladies' Championship in 1925

Photograph courtesy of Mr Alastair McIntosh

Golf increased in popularity for both men and women to such an extent that in 1923 the secretary of GGC discussed with GLGC ways of reducing the congestion on No. 1. The agreement with GGC as to playing rights was modified with GLGC paying 30/– for each member who wanted the privilege of playing over No. 1 instead of 5/– per month or 10/– for 6 months. It has not been recorded whether this rise in cost had the desired effect.

Some of the members during this period were among the most prominent players in Scotland. Mrs J.B.Watson, Mrs W.H. Nicolson, Miss Mary Wood, Mrs H Percy, Miss Doris Park, Miss M. Couper, Mrs A M Holm and Miss M M Robertson Durham were all Scottish Ladies' Champions in the twenties and thirties.

"In 1927 four of Scotland's best women players entered for the "Dispatch" Trophy and sent hundreds scurrying up to the Hill [Braid Hills Golf Club] *to watch what happened.*

Representing the Dormie Club that May day were Mrs J.B. Watson and Miss Mary Wood; Doris Park with Edith Nimmo. In these days no stronger women's team could have been fielded. There were three Scottish champions in that distinguished line up and Edith Nimmo was eight times club champion at Dalmahoy. ...Their opponents that day were Moray House...who won on the last green... The women might have done better had they been better acquainted with the course and of the requirements of double foursome play.

Mind you the women never got another chance to learn. The rules of the tournament were changed the following year barring them"

Ian Macniven, The Evening News, 1968

From 1926 the energies of GLGC were directed to developing a new Clubhouse with GGC. As the development was to be on the site of GLGC's Clubhouse an agreement between GLGC and GGC was made in 1928.

1928 Agreement with GGC

This agreement covered many aspects of joint interest to the two clubs: membership subscriptions and numbers, playing rights, clubhouse facilities and maintenance. It has been of fundamental importance to the two Clubs in any negotiations they have had with each other.

GLGC transferred ownership of their ground and clubhouse to GGC. The members did not receive any money but certain arrangements were made for their benefit.

They had exclusive use of a Club Room and Dressing Room with lockers and other necessary conveniences; the use of a common Dining Room and Lounge; the right to play over the Gullane Golf Courses; a separate outside entrance.

The subscription to be paid by a full member of GLGC was 2/3rds of the subscription paid by a full member of GGC. This was to be increased pro rata as necessary but the Ladies were to be given a year's notice of any increase. The Ladies had to furnish their own rooms and to pay a share of furnishing the common rooms. GGC would pay for the installation and maintenance of the lighting and heating plant.

The management and control of the Courses and Clubhouse was vested solely in GGC with the exception of the rooms reserved for the exclusive use of GLGC.

The minimum number of GLGC members was to be 200. The maximum was not specified in the agreement. However at the AGM of GLGC in November 1928 it was agreed that the membership of the Club be limited to 250 to avoid overcrowding in the new Clubhouse.

The three members representing GLGC were Mrs Beatrix Pitman, Captain in 1928, Miss Elizabeth Robertson Durham, secretary and Miss May Lennox whose brother Hugh was GLGC's lawyer. Representing GGC were Mr Alex. Robertson Durham, Sir Harold Stiles and Mr Benjamin Hall Blyth. Mr Alex Robertson Durham was the father of Miss Elizabeth Robertson Durham; Sir Harold Stiles' daughter, Mrs Rome was Captain in 1929 and Mrs Hall Blyth had been Captain in 1925.

There were many close connections between the Clubs and it might have seemed obvious to link them together at this stage. However this was not done. Instead a clear agreement was made which is still in force.

The Thirties, 1930–1939

Golf fast increased in popularity and the 250 limit was soon reached and a waiting list formed. The congestion on the waiting list in 1930 was discussed by the Committee. The first priority was to ensure that members' daughters would be able to get membership so 50% of each year's vacancies were to be filled by them. At this stage there were two classes of members – those wanting the right to play on Nos. 1,2 and 3 and those who only wanted to play on Nos. 2 and 3.

In 1931 a further proposal was to create a class of Non Playing Membership for older members. This meant that those members who became Non Playing would vacate a "space" in the membership numbers for a new member. This has been most successful and in the present day there is steady movement each year towards Non Playing Membership. There were 26 in this category in 2002.

In 1931 there was much discussion as to how new members should be elected. Again this has been a regular topic over the years. Up to that time members were proposed, seconded and then elected by a Committee Ballot. The proposal in 1931 was that the election of new members should be changed from a Committee Ballot to a Club Ballot. No candidate was to be admitted if fewer than 10 members voted for her. Adverse votes counted towards exclusion. This method was only tried twice before the Committee decided to reverse the decision as it had proved a failure owing to abuse by members! The actual form of the abuse was not recorded although one can imagine the system was open to vote rigging. The Committee ballot evolved to the process today of putting a candidate's name up on display for a month and if no one objects the candidate's name is added to the waiting list.

The Committee also requested that GLGC be allowed to increase membership to 300. This was refused by GGC in 1932 and was not reconsidered until after the Second World War when it was agreed in 1946 that GLGC could have 300 full playing members.

In the 30's golf was a casual affair with much emphasis also being placed on the playing of bridge. Indeed one of the Life Honorary Members, Mrs Robertson who joined as Miss Hall Blyth in the 1920s, recalls that you wore your old clothes to golf. She is amazed at how smart some of today's golfers are. In 1958 Mrs Isobel Hastings was invited by her future mother-in-law to play a mixed foursomes at Gullane. She was firmly instructed to wear a skirt on the golf course as trousers were not considered suitable wear for Gullane Ladies.

The War Years, 1939–45

During the war the courses were neglected to a large degree.

" In 1939 the game at Gullane came virtually to a standstill. Players disappeared. The green keeping staff was whittled down to four elderly men. No 2 and No 3 courses were not maintained, except for the greens on No 2 which were mown whenever possible. But actual playing on both courses ceased. The military took over large areas for defence purposes. Searchlights, gun posts, pits, miles of barbed wire – all the paraphernalia of coastal defence – invaded the former peaceful fairways. Other areas were marked for training purposes.

During this period of military activity, the No 1 course was fortunate to be left alone to a large extent. The authorities showed refreshing consideration and the greens escaped damage. But there were some casualties... ...The winding line of concrete anti tank obstacles engulfed the twelfth hole from tee to green.. ...Greens became weedy. Bunkers were in a sorry plight.

The rot was stopped largely through the energy and initiative of Mrs Beddows, better known as Mrs J.B. Watson, who organised working parties of elderly club members and lady members to go out on the course for weeding and bunker exercises. This timely intervention undoubtedly went a long way towards simplifying the present work of getting the course back to good condition."

Golf Illustrated June 5th 1947

At the end of the war the concrete blocks on the twelfth hole presented a real problem:

" In places four deep, they stood about 6 feet high—with a couple of feet or so below the surface- and roughly five feet apart. Each block weighed approximately six and a half tons. An estimate showed that over 200 would have to be shifted from the twelfth fairway of the No.1 course"

Golf Illustrated June 5th 1947

Gullane provided a novel solution: the blocks should be buried. At the Ladies' Amateur Championship held in 1947 over No. 1 scarcely a trace remained of this mass burial. How many players today realise they are walking over these blocks?

Golf Illustrated 1947
courtesy of David Kirkwood

1946– Present Day

After the war attitudes changed; GLGC took on new life and attracted some of the most prominent lady golfers of the day as members. Their achievements have been prodigious and have enhanced the status of GLGC to its position today. Indeed Mrs Pat Hendry, a Life Honorary Member, recalls that when she got married in 1946 to a good golfer she was instructed to join GLGC as her husband said that if you want to play serious women's golf you have to join Gullane Ladies. There was no other option!

In 1946 the 300 full Members were exclusive of Non Playing Members, Members resident abroad and Honorary Members. During the War Years wives of Service Members and ladies temporarily resident in Gullane were admitted as annual Members but this privilege was stopped after the War.

However in the immediate aftermath of the war the number of members dropped. This was no doubt due to petrol rationing and general lack of money. In 1957 there were 263 members including Country Members. GGC was having similar problems at the time and there was considerable cooperation between the Clubs with GLGC giving extra funds to help GGC with the costs of running the Club as has been detailed earlier.

Numbers increased rapidly in the late seventies and early eighties. The 300 mark was easily reached and the waiting list lengthened quickly. To counteract this problem different categories of membership have been introduced.

From the beginning of the Club many of the members of GLGC have been of doughty character and have a robust approach to life as typified by the following anecdotes.

"Mrs Audrey Morrison was riding her horse among the Gullane bents when a naked man suddenly sprang out in front of her. Totally unfazed she merely remarked "Oh dear. Aren't you cold?" and rode on."

Mrs Gill Morrison, Member

"In 1983, four members, Mrs Judy Cuthbertson, Mrs Shona Low, Mrs Maureen Matthews and Mrs Margaret Sneddon played 72 holes in one day to raise money for St Columba's Hospice. The courses played were Kilspindie, Gullane No. 2, Gullane No 1 and finally Gullane No. 3. They started at 6 a.m. and finished at 7p.m with enough energy for a party in the Clubhouse afterwards. They raised £1200."

Margaret Sneddon, Captain 2001–2002

"Mrs Marguerite Roberts, Captain 1975–76, now aged in her late 80s, still drives two or three times each week from her home in Selkirk to play at Gullane— a drive of about an hour—even in winter!"

Country Membership

Country Membership was introduced in 1955 with their numbers included in the 300 members quota. The original purpose was to encourage those members living at a distance to retain their membership by reducing their subscription. Geographically anyone living outside the counties of Lothians, Peebles and Berwick could become a Country Member. This was increased to a 75 mile radius in 1963 but in 1976 this was changed back to a radius of 50 miles. As the mobility of people increased and as the desire to retain members reduced the Committee felt that this distance was too near and was easily achievable in one day so that those members should pay the full subscription. In 1992 it was increased again to 100 miles.

Five Day Membership

Five Day membership was introduced in 1963 with 35 Five Day members allowed outside the quota of 300. The conditions for a member to become a Five Day Member have changed over the years according to the conditions at the time and have been the subject of much lively discussion.

Originally this category was open to all members but priority was to be given to new local candidates. Over the years this changed to restrict Five Day Membership to residents of Gullane only.

In 1997, the waiting list was reformed and reopened. New candidates were put on a new list where age and place of residence were taken into consideration. This effectively allowed local candidates, who were on the waiting list, to be offered every second place. This led in 2000 to the removal of geographic restrictions on Five Day Membership. In 2002 the number of Five Day Members was increased to 40 .

Junior Membership

In 1952 it was decided that Junior Members should pay reduced subscriptions – again probably to help with family finances. They could join at age fifteen and there was to be a maximum of twenty Juniors. They would pay the Full Member's subscription at eighteen but the Entrance Fee would only be payable at twenty one. They had the same privileges as senior members on the course and in the clubhouse.

A demand for even younger players to be accepted resulted in Juvenile Membership being introduced in 1959 . Juveniles were aged 13 and 14 and could play on Nos. 2 & 3. They were only allowed into the locker room, not the main rooms in the Clubhouse. In 1991 the category of Juvenile Member was abolished.

At present any young person, usually 12 or over, can become a Junior Member immediately. The maximum number was increased to 25 in 2002.

Juniors and Committee in 1992

LtoR back: Sally Tait, Anne McKenzie, Jean Main, Gail Main, Margaret Sneddon, Ethel Jack, Katie Low
Front: Maureen Matthews, Elise Guy, Shonagh McEwan, Helen Osler, Lesley Nicholson, Cath Tait

The Waiting List

The "Post War Baby Boom" arrived at GLGC – in common with most other golf clubs– in the late seventies and eighties. These candidates were then in their thirties and early forties and beginning to find more time for golf after bringing up their families. The waiting list lengthened to such an extent that it was closed in 1989 as it was felt that new candidates would have to wait an unacceptable length of time.

In 1997 an analysis of the membership of the Club was carried out and it was found that 82% were over fifty and 48% over sixty. The Captain, Mrs Ethel Jack, and the Committee felt that this was leading to stultification in the club.

Vigorous efforts were made to find a better system that would allow the waiting list to reopen and at the same time try to redress the problems of age distribution, the size of the waiting list and the number of local and other members. All members were asked for ideas and they responded magnificently with about sixty five sending in their own suggestions. Needless to say there were many different options proposed but the final proposals formed from the suggestions went through easily at the AGM.

The waiting list now has different categories based on age and geographic location which it is hoped will counteract the ageing of the membership while preserving the Club's traditional geographic spread between locals, Edinburgh based members and those from further afield.

Babe Zaharias winning the British Ladies' Amateur Championship at Gullane in 1947

HONORARY MEMBERS

Since 1930 GLGC has had a tradition of offering Honorary Membership to people who have made a significant contribution to the Club and to golf in general. The Honorary Members elected by GLGC since the beginning of the Club are

1930	Lady Derby
1938	Lady Bingham
1945	Mrs J.L. Murray (nee Minnie Robertson Durham)
1947	Mrs Babe Zaharias
1952	Miss Moira Paterson (now Mrs Moira Milton)
	Mrs Wallace Williamson (nee Milligan)
	Miss Jean Donald (became Mrs Jean Anderson)
1956	Mrs Charlotte Beddows (nee Stevenson, then Mrs J.B. Watson)

	Miss Marjory Druitt
1964	Mrs Helen Holm
1965	Miss May Lennox
1966	Mrs Elizabeth Bowhill (nee Robertson Durham)
1971	Mrs Marjorie Draper (nee Thomas, then Mrs Peel)
1972	Mrs Dorothy Rome (nee Stiles)
1975	Mrs Elsie Mackie
1991	Mrs Patricia Hay
	Miss Elizabeth McLarty
1993	Miss Catriona Lambert (now Mrs Catriona Matthew)
	Mrs Jean Burnett
2001	Miss Connie Lugton

Lady Derby

Lady Derby was invited to become an Honorary Member in 1930. Her husband, Lord Derby had given enormous support for both GGC and GLGC in many ways.
She was delighted to accept the honour.

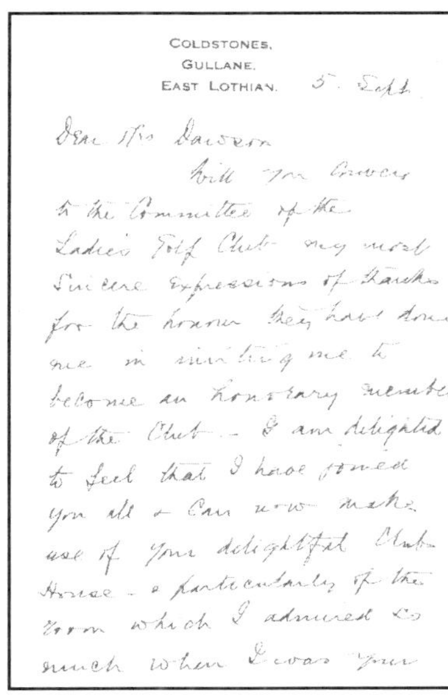
COLDSTONES,
GULLANE,
EAST LOTHIAN. 5. Sept

Dear Mrs Dawson
Will you convey to the Committee of the Ladies Golf Club my most sincere expressions of thanks for the honour they have done me in inviting me to become an honorary member of the Club. I am delighted to feel that I have joined you all & can now make use of your delightful Club House & particularly of the room which I admired so much when I was your

Lady Bingham

In 1938 the Club wanted to invite Lady Bingham to become an Honorary Member. Lady Bingham was the wife of Sir Albert Bingham who presented the Jubilee Challenge Trophy in 1935. She presented the Lady Bingham Salver for the annual Mixed Foursomes competition for members of the two clubs in 1939.

Miss Marjory Druitt, Honorary Secretary, decided to write to Major Smith, Honorary Secretary of GGC, to see whether this caused any problems as the number of members had been restricted to 250 in 1928. He replied that

"There is no restriction mentioned regarding your club making Honorary members. There is of course a definite restriction in the number of your members who are allowed to play over No 1 course"

Letter from Major Smith 1938

As Lady Bingham did not play golf there was no problem. Since then GLGC confirm that any proposed Honorary Member is acceptable to GGC.

Mrs John Murray
nee Minnie Robertson Durham
1908- 1965

Minnie Robertson Durham was a member of the Robertson Durham family who were so influential in the development of GLGC. She won the Scottish Ladies' Amateur Championship in 1935 and represented Scotland in 1936 and 37.

As Miss M. Robertson Durham she captained GLGC in 1936 -37 just before her sister Mrs Ian Bowhill. Although she served on the Committee during the war she resigned from it in 1945 after her marriage to a merchant seaman, known to everyone as "Sailor", when she went to live in Swansea. Mrs Murray was elected an Honorary member in 1945 and died in 1965.

" The most remarkable thing about her championship, however, is that she had not yet fully recovered from the skiing accident she suffered in Switzerland in February, when she broke her right leg just above the ankle. ..and yet, some four months after that mishap, she has, by an impressive exhibition of golf skill and temperament, played herself into the role of native champion

All through the event which her golf crowned this afternoon, she has worn a boot on her right foot to support her weak limb; but, apart from feeling tired at the end of each day's play, she tells me that she has really suffered no serious handicap."

Daily Express June 14th 1935

Miss Minnie Robertson Durham after winning the Scottish Ladies' Amateur Championship in 1935

Photo courtesy of SLGA

Mrs Babe Zaharias nee Didrickson 1914–1956

Mildred 'Babe' Zaharias has a special place in the history of Gullane Ladies' Golf Club. She came over from the States to compete in the British Ladies' Championship at Gullane in June 1947 partly because she had won all the major championships in America.

She was born in 1914 and was an exceptional woman athlete - her prowess at baseball earned her the nickname of "The Babe". As an 18 year old, in the 1932 Olympic Games, she established three world records for women: 80 metres Hurdle (11.3 secs.), Javelin (143 feet) and High Jump (5ft. $5^3/_4$ ins).

On giving up athletics she took up golf and very quickly dominated Women's Championships winning, among

Mrs Babe Zaharias in "her pants"

Gullane children besieging "The Babe" for her autograph

many others, the US National Women's Amateur in 1946 and the British Ladies' Championship in 1947. She turned professional in 1947 and won the US National Women's Open in 1948, 1949 and 1950. She was voted Women Athlete of the Year in 1932, 45, 46, 47 and 1950. In 1950 she was voted the Greatest Female Athlete of the half century.

The impact she made in Gullane in 1947 was much the same as Tiger Woods makes today. She arrived well in advance of the Championship and stayed at the Marine Hotel, now the Scottish Fire Training School. There were crowds everywhere she went, school children wanting her autograph and the Press besieging her for interviews. Her custom was to walk down the Main Street and vault easily over the fence surrounding the first tee much to the amazement of the onlookers.

As part of her preparation for the Championship she played a round over Gullane No1 with Mrs Dolly Rome, the Captain and Mrs Thorburn Brown.
Mr Rome and his son in law, Mr Donald McIntosh, then invited her to play at Muirfield and were so astonished at her length that they were convinced that whoever beat her would win.

She was an extrovert who enjoyed playing to the gallery with trick shots and wise cracks. After her second round win of 4 & 2 over Mrs Enid Shepherd she decided to entertain the gallery. She put a kitchen match behind her ball on the 17th tee and when she hit off it sounded like a small cannon being fired - the ball landed in one of the bunkers in front of the green. She then balanced one ball on

Jessie Valentine, Jean Donald, Babe Zaharias, Jacqueline Gordon after the British Ladies' Championship in 1947 at Gullane

top of the other in the bunker and when she hit the shot the top ball went into her pocket and the bottom ball landed on the green and went into the hole! This caused an uproar from the gallery. However this performance was frowned upon by the powers that be as, the next day, a notice was posted saying "Please do not play the by–holes".

She played Jean Donald, a member of GLGC and the reigning Scottish Champion in the semi final in an eagerly awaited match. The Babe revelled in the size of the crowd and was inspired, winning by 7 & 5 finishing an extraordinary 5 under 4s. She celebrated her win by dancing the Highland Fling on the green.

In the final she played Jacqueline Gordon from Middlesex with an estimated three thousand spectators. For the morning round the Babe had worn a grey flannel skirt for the first time in the competition as in 1947 trousers were not considered suitable for ladies playing golf. After the first 18 holes they were all square, round in 75. She then changed back into her pale blue trousers saying "they've been asking me where are ma pants?" She went on to win by 5 & 4. In the six rounds of the competition she lost only four holes. This was the first time the British Ladies' Trophy was taken to the USA.

Jenny Antonio, past captain of GLGC, competed in the Championship. She recalls that, although at first the older members were not pleased when "The Babe" played trick shots to entertain the gallery, at the end of the week they were as captivated by her as everyone else.

She was made an Honorary Member of the Club in the same year, 1947. Sadly Babe Zaharias died of cancer in 1956 at the age of 45. Her husband, George, presented her putter to the Club and it hangs in a place of honour in the Ladies' Lounge.

In the early 1960's George Zaharias gave Mr Bennett, the local headmaster, money to buy a trophy in memory of The Babe. The Babe Zaharias Trophy was first played for in 1964 and is a stroke play competition played over No. 3, open to boys and girls attending Gullane Primary School. So far, no girl has ever won!

Babe Zaharias' putter in the Ladies' lounge

Photo by Joyce Murdoch

Mrs Moira Milton
nee Moira Paterson
1923–

Moira Paterson won the British Ladies' Championship in 1952 - an achievement equalled by only two other members of GLGC - after beating Frances Stephens in the final at Troon on the 39th hole.

"When there is a local element involved, the habitual watcher can tell from the way the gallery moves how the game is going. An instance of this was when Moira Paterson defeated Miss Frances Stephens at the thirty ninth hole in the final of the British Championship at Troon. At one time Miss Paterson (the local) was well down, but as she recovered the gallery quickened their pace and before the end of the game they had started to run between shots."

A Gallery of Women Golfers. Enid Wilson

She was made an Honorary Member in 1952 having become a member of GLGC in 1948. Catriona Matthew is the only other Honorary Member surviving.

Among Moira's other championship wins are the Dumbartonshire in 1949, East of Scotland in 1960 and Midlothian in 1962. She was runner up for the French title in 1949 and in the Scottish Ladies' Championship in 1951 having reached the semi finals in 1950.

She played for Scotland in the Home Internationals in 1949–50–52 and was a member of the winning Curtis Cup team at Muirfield in 1952 when GB and I won by 5 matches to 4. When the Ladies Golf Union sent a touring team to South Africa in 1951 Moira Paterson was included along with Jean Anderson. She played against France in 1949 and 1951 and against Australia in 1951.

Moira particularly remembers being Vice Captain of Scotland when Miss Elizabeth McLarty was Captain for about four years. They were very happy days for her and she found the girls in the team delightful. Her final international honours came in 1973 when she was non–playing Captain of Scotland.

Mrs Wallace Williamson nee Milligan 1894 – 1972

Miss Milligan was one of the first members of the Club and her future administrative ability was recognised early as she was elected to the Committee in 1912, aged 18. Her mother had been one of the fourteen founding members present at Dowells' Rooms in 1904. When Miss Stiles resigned as Honorary Secretary in 1918 Miss Milligan took over until 1925. After marrying Mr R.H. Wallace Williamson in 1919 she became affectionately known as "Wally Willy"

As Secretary she was very involved in the negotiations for the feu of Shepherd's Cottage in the early twenties and worked hard with Mr Hugh Lennox, the Club's lawyer, to ensure that the terms of the Feu Charter were the best for the Club.

She was involved in some controversy at the Club in 1928 when she and two other of the most prominent members, Mrs J. B. Watson and Miss Park, played in a three ball at a medal. The Committee decided that they should be disqualified but the three players disagreed and appealed to the LGU for a ruling on whether their scores should stand. There was some irony in this as Mrs Wallace Williamson was the Handicap Manager of the Club appointed by the LGU. The ruling was in their favour but it certainly occasioned much discussion as evidenced in the minutes.

After the only ballot for Captain that the Club has held, as detailed in the chapter on the Club Management, "Wally Willy" became Captain of the Club in 1934–35. A top class player, she won the East of Scotland Ladies' Championship in 1935 having been runner up in 1932. She played for Scotland in the Home Internationals in 1932 and for the British Ladies' v. France in 1935 and v. Canada in 1938. She was non playing Captain of the Curtis Cup team in 1938.

She contributed immensely to the administration of golf becoming Chairman of the Executive Council of the LGU in 1948- 49.

She was made an Honorary member of the Club in 1952 and died in 1972.

Mrs Jean Anderson nee Donald 1921— 1984

Jean Donald was born in North Berwick. Her golfing achievements were prodigious and many members at GLGC still remember her with great affection.

She was Captain of the Club from 1951 –52 at the early age of 30 and was Honorary Secretary from 1966 –68. Just before she relinquished her amateur status in 1953 she was made an Honorary Member of the Club. She enjoyed the life of a professional but complained that there was a lack of tournaments in which she could

Jean Donald after winning the Scottish Ladies' Championship in 1947

play. She would willingly have foregone any prize just to be allowed to compete.

In 1947 Babe Zaharias beat her in the semi finals of the British Ladies' Championship at Gullane. Although her record in the British Amateur was excellent, reaching the semi finals in 1946–47– 51 –53 and runner up in 1948, she never won the title. She won other championships many times; the Scottish Ladies' Championship in 1947–49–52, a runner up in 1953 and a semi finalist in 1951; the French Ladies' Open Championship in 1947; the East of Scotland Ladies' Championship in 47–48–49–53 and the East Lothian Ladies' Championship in 1948–49–51–52–53. She won the Sunningdale Open Foursomes four times – first with T.B. Haliburton in 1951 and 53 and then with Peter Alliss in 1958 and 61. Internationally she played in the Curtis Cup in 1948–50–52; against France in 1947–48–49–51–53; against Belgium in 1949–51–53; against New Zealand in 1953. She toured South Africa as a member of the Ladies' Golf Union team in 1951. She played for Scotland in the Home Internationals from 1947 to 1953.

Jean Donald playing at Muirfield in the Curtis Cup in 1952

Many of the members of GLGC remember Jean with great affection as she had a huge personality who made younger and new members feel very welcome at the Club. Although she was certainly unconventional she was an inspiration to lady golfers for many years, particularly to the younger generation. As one of GLGC Past Captains, Jenny Antonio, recalls

"One day I had put on a new pair of shoes (a mistake!) and by the 3rd hole I had blisters so on Jean's recommendations I played in my bare feet. Playing with Jean we were often told to play

through and I hesitate to think what the men thought of Jean's partner!"

Jenny Antonio, Captain 1985–86

In 1948 the press referred to her as a "sartorial sensation" when she wore waterproof trousers in the final of the 1948 British Ladies' Championship. She was described at this time as one of the successes of post war golf. Although she took up an appointment with Golf Ball Development as a representative in 1949 this did not affect her amateur status. When she did turn professional in 1953 this was described as a "severe blow to Scotland". She gave her name to a set of clubs—Jean Donald —which became extremely popular and are still used by many ladies today.

She loved playing at Gullane and is recorded as saying:

"On a clear day there can be very few views as magnificent as the one from the 7th tee. From this tee one gets a complete panoramic picture.

"There can be few scenes more beautiful on an August evening than the sight from the 17th tee of the golden fields ready for harvesting to the south of the village.

"It is at times difficult to concentrate on the golf, for combined with the magnificent scenery, one has to contend with the sound of skylarks and the peewits and the occasional raucous noise of a cock pheasant.

"One is very conscious of the history of Gullane. So many people have played these links. I was fortunate to play as long ago as 1946 in a foursome with James Braid, one of the great triumvirate. What an education that was! In the foursome was Mrs Charlotte Beddows, one of Gullane's most famous personalities. In 1947 I played with the amazing

Babe Zaharias, These golfers are, alas, no longer with us but are part of golfing history."
Jean Donald, Captain 1951–52

She died very suddenly at the club in 1984 - just a few weeks after her husband. Her family left her medals and trophies to GLGC and they are still displayed in a special cabinet, gifted by her sisters, in the Ladies' lounge. Her Australian friends arranged for a seat to be put on the course overlooking the 11th green and with the magnificent views she loved.

Jean Donald's trophies in the Ladies' Lounge

Photo by Joyce Murdoch

Mrs Charlotte Beddows
was Mrs J.B. Watson
nee Stevenson
1887–1976

Charlotte Beddows was one of life's enthusiasts who just loved to play golf—she played every day if she possibly could. She had a long and very distinguished golfing career being one of the most remarkable golfers of the 20th Century and a major influence in Scottish Ladies' golf. She generously donated a large number of trophies to various ladies' golf clubs and associations and recognised the importance of the development of Junior Golf. She lived in Gullane and was a member of many clubs besides Gullane.

The statistics which relate to Mrs Beddows' golfing career are amazing. She was seventeen when she won the Bronze Medal at the 1905 Scottish Women's Championship. Forty five years later she was a finalist at St Andrews. Altogether she won the title four times, in 1920–21–22–29, and was twice runner up in 1923 and in 1950. She won the Scottish Veteran Ladies' Championship four times in five years – in 1947–49–50–51.

One of her greatest prides was the number of years she represented Scotland in the Home Internationals – 21 times between 1913 and 1951 notwithstanding two World Wars during this period. The unofficial matches between Great Britain and the United States had been such a success that a formal contest was inaugurated in 1932, the winners to hold a trophy provided by the Curtis sisters of America - the Curtis Cup. Mrs Beddows played in the first Curtis Cup side in 1932 at Wentworth when she was forty five years old. She also played in the first Vagliano Trophy match between Britain and France in 1931.

She first represented East Lothian in 1909, aged 22, and made her last appearance for her county in 1966 when aged 78. At the age of 77 when playing over Longniddry she did the first seven holes on the inward half in the remarkable figures 4,4,4,3,5,4,2. In November 1971 when she was 84 years old she holed a No 3 wood at the 5th hole on Gullane No 2 - the 7th hole–in–one of her career. At the age of 80 she played off a handicap of 8.

Her speed of play was legendary. Marjory Ferguson recalled playing a Club Championship tie against her where they were round in under two hours, partly because, as a result of her reputation for fast play, everyone stood back and invited them to come through.

"Mrs Beddows never walks, she goes round at a rate the army would call 'quick time' and the navy would term 'at the double'"

Enid Wilson. A Gallery of Women Golfers

The contribution she made to golf was immense. Among her achievements she was Captain of the British team v. France in 1939 and of the Scottish team in 1921–22–23–30–31. She was President of the Scottish Ladies' Golf Association five times and deservedly won the Frank Moran Trophy, awarded annually to a Scot who has done most for golf, in 1964.

Charlotte Beddows excelled in another sport - hockey. Enid Wilson, in her book "A Gallery of Women Golfers" opines that the reason why Mrs Beddows was exceptionally good with her irons was that she had been a hockey internationalist. Before 1914 she had captained the Scottish Team and had played in 18 international matches. She was President of the Scottish Women's Hockey Association from 1925–1931.

Very few people realised that she suffered from polio in 1955 but refused to allow it to affect her golf. Her caddy, Doddy Moran, looked after her steadfastly. He used to hold her finger as she was walking between shots to keep it warm.

Although she was wont to arrive at competitions in her Jaguar, driven by her chauffeur/caddie, she was not renowned for a "soft" approach to life. She refused to have central heating in her home and would have her daily game of golf no matter what the weather.

She was a formidable character at the golf club. Miss Bobby Sharpe recalls playing a Winter Foursome tie partnered by her sister Marjorie Sharpe against Mrs Beddows and her partner on a particularly cold day. At the ninth hole Mrs Beddows suggested that they needed a little something to keep out the cold. It was a little disappointing to be given two ginger snap biscuits! Christian Thin remembers that she always had a chat or joke with her and her cousins in passing them while they were playing on the Children's Course - she strongly believed in encouraging youngsters to play.

As has been written earlier it was greatly due to her efforts that No 1 was reinstated to such good condition so quickly after the end of World War II Charlotte joined GLGC in 1925 and was made an Honorary Member in 1956.

Miss Marjory Druitt
1901– 1995

Miss Marjory Druitt was a stalwart member of GLGC who gave many years of devoted service. She joined the Club in 1926 and became Honorary Secretary in 1930. She remained in this post until 1960. After her successor, Mrs Angela McIntosh, took ill she took over again as Honorary Secretary for 1963–65. Not only did she perform this onerous task she was Honorary Treasurer from 1933 until 1976. She was Captain in 1961–62 and was made an Honorary Member in 1960.

She is remembered with great affection at the club. Mrs Ethel Jack said of her that she was a charming lady; very quiet but just loved to do work for GLGC.

Mrs Helen Holm
1907–1971

Helen Holm, one of the greatest Scottish women golfers, is associated mostly with the West of Scotland. Perhaps as a consequence of her friendship with Mrs Dolly Rome she joined GLGC in 1945 and was made an Honorary Member in 1964.

She won the Scottish title five times (between 1932 and 1950) and was runner–up also five times. She was British Women's Champion twice in 1934 and in 1938, and was a Curtis Cup member three times (she declined to travel to the States for other Curtis Cups because her son was an infant).

Her opponent in the 1950 Scottish final was Charlotte Beddows, then aged 62, and already a four–times previous winner.

Photo courtesy of SLGA

Miss May Lennox
–1971

Miss May Lennox was one of the original members of the Club. She was Captain in 1913 and Treasurer from 1923—1931. She presented the silver Captains Board in 1965 when she was made an Honorary Member. She died in 1971.

Christine Lessels has a childhood memory of having tea with Miss Lennox at Margrie

"She was tall, quietly spoken and rather old fashioned. She had been captain of games at her boarding school which she was sure I would enjoy if I also liked games."

Christine Lessels Vice Captain 2003-04

Mrs Elizabeth Bowhill
nee Robertson Durham
1906 –1967

Mrs Bowhill at the Scottish Ladies' Amateur in 1937

Photo courtesy of SLGA

Mrs Bowhill made a huge contribution to the Club. As Elizabeth Robertson Durham she was Honorary Secretary during the crucial years while GLGC was negotiating the 1928 Agreement with GGC. She was Captain from 1937 - 46 and steered the Club through the War Years. To help the Club through this difficult time she worked there behind the bar although she herself only drank ginger beer.

GLGC had tried to increase the number of members allowed in the early thirties but it was not until 1946 when Mrs Bowhill was Captain that negotiations with GGC resulted in an increase in the maximum number of members of GLGC. Those negotiations were perhaps made easier as her husband Mr Ian Bowhill was Captain of GGC at the time.

She was also an excellent golfer – she was runner up in the Scottish Ladies' Amateur in 1937 at Gleneagles and played for Scotland in 1938. She was made an Honorary Member in 1966 but sadly died the following year.

Mrs Marjorie Draper
was Mrs Peel
nee Thomas
1905–1988

Marjorie Draper was another of the outstanding Scottish lady golfers who have been members of GLGC. Gullane was her home club and she loved playing there all her life. She was Captain of Gullane Ladies' Golf Club in 1948–50 and was made an Honorary Member in 1971.

She won the Scottish Ladies' Championship in 1954 and the East of Scotland championship seven times between 1951 and 1961. Her international honours began by representing Scotland in 1929 then thirteen more times with her last appearance in 1962. She was a member of the Curtis Cup team which played at Merion, USA in 1954 and she played for Britain against France and Belgium in 1955. She won the Worplesdon Foursomes with Mr. G.W. Mackie in 1952. As Marjorie Thomas she played for GLGC in the winning Eglinton Quaich team in 1924 and 25 then later on, as Mrs Peel, in 1934, then 1949 onwards until 1959.

Her captaincy skills were legendary. She was the non playing Captain of the Curtis Cup team and of the Vagliano Trophy team in 1963; of Scotland in 1961–63 -65. The members of the International teams when she was captain said that she was one of the best captains they ever had. She was also very involved with golf administration and was President of Scottish Ladies' Golfing Association from 1973–75.

She was a well known golfer in Scotland. When she was playing at Aberdour with Joan Lawrence later in her career as Mrs Draper she got stuck in a rather deep bunker at the first. Her caddie said "the only woman who could get out of there was Marjorie Thomas". A voice was heard coming from the bunker " I AM Marjorie Thomas"!

She was not averse to a bit of gamesmanship. A Muirfield member recalls playing against her in a foursomes in a Pirates Match. He and his partner were doing quite well until Mrs Draper asked him "What is your handicap?" After the requisite reply she then commented, "Oh, I thought it would be much more than that!" Mrs Draper and her partner won! Again one of our members recalled that one day Mrs Draper said to her that Gullane needed a good practice ground. The member replied " Doesn't bother me. I never use a practice ground". Response from Mrs Draper " And it shows."

Connie Lugton was playing with her one day when she was in the rough at the left hand side of the 17th hole. She stood back from addressing her ball and said to Connie " I'm telling you now in case you think it's a fluke shot. I'm aiming at the space between the bunkers because I can't carry them." She duly hit the shot between the bunkers and finished beside the hole.

She instigated the Peel Trophy competition. It was first played in 1950 on Gullane No 3 and is a hole and hole competition for both girls and boys divided into two age groups. Since it started it has been a well known feature of the summer's golf in East Lothian. It is currently organised by Liz Beak with donations from a variety of people including GLGC.

A painting by Kenneth Robertson, which hangs in the Ladies' Lounge, was commissioned in her memory.

Gullane Golf Course by Kenneth Robertson in memory of Mrs Draper. It hangs in the Ladies' Lounge

Mrs. Dolly Rome
nee Stiles
1895 -1977

Photo courtesy of Alastair McIntosh

Mrs Rome was born Miss Dorothy Stiles and was the daughter of Sir Harold Stiles, a prominent gynaecologist in the early part of the century. She became Honorary Secretary of GLGC in 1913, aged 18, taking over from Mrs R.M. Watson. However , after her marriage to Mr S.G. Rome in 1918 she resigned and Miss Milligan, later Mrs Wallace Williamson, took over.

She became Captain of the Club in 1929 and together with Miss Elizabeth Robertson Durham, then Honorary Secretary, steered the Club through the days of building and furnishing the Clubhouse in 1929–30. She must have been very relieved to get all negotiations for the furnishings and fittings for the clubhouse out of the way and opened the present clubhouse in 1930 with great pleasure. She donated the Championship Cup in memory of her father and gifted the Club flag whenever it needed to be renewed.

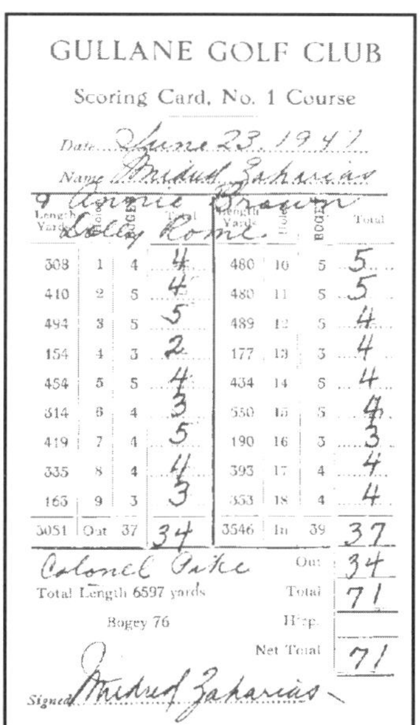

GULLANE GOLF CLUB

Scoring Card, No. 1 Course

Date June 23, 1947

Name Mildred Zaharias

Annie Brown

Dolly Rome

Length Yards	Hole	Bogey	Total	Length Yards	Hole	Bogey	Total
308	1	4	4	480	10	5	5
410	2	5	4	480	11	5	5
494	3	5	5	489	12	5	4
154	4	3	2	177	13	3	4
454	5	5	4	434	14	5	4
314	6	4	3	530	15	5	4
419	7	4	5	190	16	3	3
335	8	4	4	393	17	4	4
165	9	3	3	353	18	4	4
3051	Out	37	34	3546	In	39	37

Colonel Oake

Out 34

Total Length 6597 yards — Total 71

Bogey 76 — H'cp.

Net Total 71

Signed Mildred Zaharias

Courtesy of Derek McIntosh

She was not allowed to golf peacefully however as the Club called upon her to become Captain again in 1947–48 immediately after Mrs Elizabeth Bowhill. She is the only person to have been Captain twice. This was a time of great change for the Club as attitudes as well as material prosperity had changed so much during the War Years. It is to the great credit of these leaders that GLGC weathered these changes so successfully.

Her family stayed very involved with the golf world. Her daughter Angela McIntosh became Captain also and her granddaughter in law, Mrs Barbara McIntosh, was English Champion. Mrs Rome was made an Honorary Member in 1972 and died in 1977.

One of the best mementoes of Mrs Rome is owned by her grandson Derek McIntosh. In 1937 when she was Captain she played round Gullane No 1 with Babe Zaharias and Anne Thorburn Brown just before the British Ladies' Championship of 1947. Babe Zaharias marked her card for the game and this unique signed card is a prized possession.

Mrs Elsie Mackie
1905–96

Mrs Elsie Mackie was made an Honorary Member in 1975. She was born and brought up in Stirling where she developed her golfing skills in the 1920s and 30s, representing Stirling County.

She married Squiggles Mackie, a prominent golfer and a Captain of the R & A. She became Captain of East Lothian Ladies' Golf Association and of Gullane Ladies' Golf Club in 1955.

When GLGC started an Open Stroke Play Competition for low handicap players in 1973 they did not have a trophy until in 1974 Mrs Mackie presented a magnificent trophy for the winner. The competition, now known as The Mackie Bowl, is held annually over Gullane No. 1, and is one of the premier golfing events at the top level of ladies' amateur golf in Scotland. She supported the competition more than just financially. Each year she would entertain the Committee of the day to lunch and expected the Captain of the day to look after her. Her gin and tonics were legendary!

She was an extremely strong character with an exceptional joie de vivre who did not hesitate to say what she felt. It has to be admitted however that she never properly understood the principle of standing in a queue as she simply proceeded to its head and demanded attention. She died at the age of 90 in 1996

Mrs Patricia Hay
1913-1998

Photo courtesy of Margaret Sneddon

Mrs Patricia Hay was President of the SLGA in 1985, Captain of the GLCC in 1957 - 58 and was made an Honorary Member in 1991. An outgoing character, she had hoped to be an opera singer before her marriage. She lived in Duns Castle and was known as "The Duchess". She loved entertaining her friends with a song as well as with a "sewing machine", which went to all golf championships with her, and was full of drinks!. Her golfing friends learnt to treat her 'Duns Special Cocktail' with respect. Her hat covered with badges from around the world made her easily recognisable at golf events

Miss Elizabeth McLarty
1911-1993

Miss McLarty was Captain of the Club in 1966–68. In 1967 and 1970 she won the Scottish Veteran Ladies' Championship and was Captain of the Scottish team at the International Matches at Sunningdale in 1967 when Scotland was unbeaten. It was said that it was one of the happiest teams ever due to her excellent captaincy. She was made an Honorary Member in 1991.

Mrs Catriona Matthew
nee Lambert
1969 –

Catriona Matthew is a truly exceptional golfer. She was born in 1969 and played her golf at both Gullane Ladies' Golf Club and North Berwick. She felt that playing at GLGC, which had so many great players, really helped her improve since she had to play against many Scottish Internationalists in the monthly medals and club championship which was excellent competition for her.

"I did most of my practising at Gullane mainly because I was lucky enough to get coaching from Jimmy Hume and the putting green there was so good. I used to, and still do, try and hole 100 consecutive putts from 2/3 feet before I could go home. Sounds pretty easy but on this particular day I was struggling and it took me quite a while. I came back the next day and found that the two footprints on the green where I had been had had to be repaired, so I had a couple of days off from putting practice!"
Catriona Matthew 2003

She very quickly came to prominence winning the Scottish Girls' Championship in 1986. This was followed by wins in the Scottish Ladies' Championship in 1991, 93 and 94.

"I had the thrill of playing in my last Scottish Ladies' Amateur in 1994 at Gullane No. 1 before I turned pro. It put a little bit more pressure on me to do well as I was a member there and was the favourite. I had a great week

and was lucky enough to come out on top which was fantastic as it was in front of so many family and friends."

Catriona Matthew 2003

She won the British Ladies' Amateur Championship in 1993 as well as the Spanish Ladies' Championship. A Scottish Internationalist from 1986–1994, she played in the Curtis Cups of 1990, 92 and 94. She represented the UK in the Espirito Santo World Team Championship in 1992 and played in the Vagliano Trophy, for Britain against Europe, in 1989, 91, 93.

She turned professional in 1994 and has since won the Australian Ladies' Open Championship in 1996, the Macdonalds WPGA Championship of Europe in 1998 and the Hawaiian Ladies' Open in 2001. She has represented the UK in the Solheim Cup.

She was made an Honorary member of GLGC in 1993.

Mrs Jean Burnett
nee McDowell
1908– 2000

Mrs Burnett was made an Honorary Member in 1993. She had made a huge contribution to the administrative and organisational side of the golfing world. This culminated in her becoming President of the Scottish Ladies' Golfing Association and Vice President of the Ladies Golf Union in 1985 having been Chairman of the Executive Council from 1969–71.

An outstanding swimmer during the twenties and thirties, she represented Britain in the Olympic Games of 1928. She competed at a time when even the founder of the modern Olympic Games, Pierre de Coubertin, was strongly against women's participation in sports, but female sporting pioneers ignored the social norms of the time.

Jean Burnett never cared about the opinions of those who might want to curtail her sporting activities and used to say "I liked sports. I was good at them and I just got on with it"

This interest and enthusiasm stayed with her to the end; she could be seen regularly driving to the Gullane course to play 6 holes at 7a.m. in her 90th year.

Miss Connie Lugton
1936- 2003

Connie Lugton was one of the most influential and respected members of GLGC from the sixties until her death. The greatest pleasure in her life was the game of golf and she always said that golf had brought her many long lasting friendships which were very important to her. She had a wonderfully easy swing which was admired by everyone and envied by most.

She lived in Gullane from the age of two and was a loyal and fervent supporter of GLCC. She had a fundamental understanding of what the club stood for and could be relied on in Committee to give a wise judgement on any proposed ventures. She had often seen it all before!

Connie Lugton on winning the Scottish Ladies' Amateur in 1977
Photo courtesy of SLGA

Her achievements in the game are numerous. She won the Scottish Ladies' Championship in 1977 and was runner up in 1972. She was East of Scotland Champion in 1974 and won the East Lothian Ladies' Championship nine times between 1965 and 1980.

At the International level she was a Girl International in 1955, represented Scotland at Senior level in the Home Internationals seven times between 1965 and 1980 and was non playing Captain in 1975–76. She played in the European Team Championship in 1977. She won the Scottish Veterans' Championship in 1987.

Not all her talents lay on the golf course. She put a lot back into the game by taking on many administrative duties in spite of having a full time job in the Civil Service. At local level she was Captain and then President of the East Lothian County Ladies' Golf Association. She served on the Executive Committee of the Scottish Ladies' Golfing Association and also became a team selector.

Connie had a great love for GLGC and participated fully right up to her death. She was Captain of GLGC in 1994–96 then came back on to the Committee as the first Membership Secretary from 1997 -2002. This second job required her to master computer skills and she had great pride in the system she produced for maintaining the Waiting List records. She was made an Honorary Member in 2001.

" I think it is fair to say that Connie derived her greatest pleasure from the "friendly" golf she shared with the Dirty Dozen of which she became President. This was an elite band of very good golfers who not only played golf but shared a social life at dinners and weekends away. Her membership of the Heather Nomads, of which she was Secretary, also gave her a chance to meet golfers from all over Europe and South Africa.

My games of golf with Connie, Belinda and Margaret were the highlight of our winter weekends. The bets were 10p per 9 holes and 10p for the game - a total of 30p– but we might as well have been playing for £30,000. We loved it when it came to the end of the winter and we all took off to Spain or Portugal for a week's holiday and to play for the The Saturday Four Championship."

Ethel Jack. Captain 1997–98. 2003

Connie herself clearly remembered watching Babe Zaharias playing in the 1947 British Ladies' Championship and being inspired by her prodigious ability. Her determination to do things her way was demonstrated from an early age. When she was four years old she, together with another two little girls, decided to tricycle from Gullane up to the then dairy at Fenton Barns – a distance of about two miles along the main road. Although they were missed and had been spotted tricycling along the main road out of the village no one dreamt that they would have gone so far! However Connie safely led her friends to the dairy, had a glass of milk and tricycled back again.

Minnie Robertson Durham after winning the Scottish Ladies' Championship in 1936 with her family

LtoR: Charlotte Thomson, Captain 1924, Mabel R–D, Captain 1914, Mrs Charles Carlow, Miss Minnie R–D, Captain 36–37, Mrs Bowhill, Captain 1937–46, Miss Margaret R–D, Mrs R–D (senior), Mr Alec R–D.
Photo courtesy of Mrs Catherine Robertson Durham

MEMBERS OF NOTE

There have been many other members of GLGC who are noteworthy apart from those who have been made Honorary Members. It is difficult to make a truly comprehensive list but those who have won major championships, represented their country, participated in the national administration of Ladies' golf or who have been particularly influential at GLGC are mentioned below.

The Robertson Durhams

No history of Gullane Ladies' Golf Club could be complete without a chapter on the Robertson Durhams. It used to be said that the reason that the Clubhouse was designed with two doors was that one door was for the Robertson Durhams and the other door was for the rest. Which door was which is not clear!

James Robertson moved to Gullane in 1892 into what is Templar Lodge in the main street and added Durham to his name in 1899. He and his wife had ten children – five sons, five daughters. Many of these children, male and female, their spouses and their spouses' families were highly influential in the development of golf, both men's and ladies', in Gullane.

Three of the five Robertson Durham daughters became Captains. Two of the five sons remained in Gullane and both their wives became Captains. Two of his granddaughters and two granddaughters-in-law became Captains. His great granddaughter-in-law, an English Champion, was Handicap secretary for some years. Three of his great great granddaughters, Lucilla, Fiona and Virginia McIntosh, are members.

Many members of the families of the spouses of the Robertson Durhams also became closely involved with GLGC as can be seen from the following list of Captains with the date in which they were Captain. Their relationship with James Robertson is shown in brackets.

1914	Mrs Alec Robertson Durham nee Mabel Stevenson (daughter in law)
1921	Mrs R.W. Stevenson (daughter). May Robertson Durham married Mabel Stevenson's brother, Wilfred
1922	Miss Maudie Paul (daughter in law); married son James
1924	Mrs W. Thomson (daughter); Charlotte Robertson Durham married first Rafe Turnbull then William Thomson
1926	Mrs T. Dryborough (daughter); Emily Robertson Durham married Thomas Dryborough
1929	Mrs S.G. Rome; nee Stiles; mother –in –law of Donald McIntosh (grandson) Was made an Honorary Member
1931	Mrs A.H. Bowhill; sister in law of Mrs I. Bowhill nee Elizabeth Robertson Durham (granddaughter);
1932	Mrs P. Turnbull; sister in law of daughter Charlotte Thomson by her first marriage
1936–37	Miss M.M. Robertson Durham (granddaughter); Minnie was daughter of Alec and Mabel Stevenson; Scottish Champion in 1935. Was made an Honorary Member

1937–46	Mrs I. Bowhill (granddaughter); Elizabeth, sister of Minnie, daughter of Alec & Mabel. Was made an Honorary Member
1947–48	Mrs S.G. Rome; the only person to have been Captain twice.
1953–54	Mrs Angela McIntosh (granddaughter-in-law) married to Donald McIntosh; daughter of Mrs Rome
1977–78	Mrs Catherine Robertson Durham (granddaughter-in-law); wife of Guy who was the son of Maudie and James

The family were almost all very enthusiastic golfers.

"The open handicap tournament in ladies foursomes, organised by Mrs. S.G. Rome and Mrs. Bowhill, was concluded yesterday over the No.3 course at Gullane, the finalists being Miss Robertson Durham with Miss M.M. Robertson Durham, Gullane (4 strokes), and Mrs. R.W. Stevenson, Edinburgh with Mrs. A.S. Paul, Edinburgh (22) ....The final was almost a Robertson Durham affair, the Misses Robertson Durham being nieces of Mrs. Stevenson, one of the winners, and Mrs. Paul, the other winner being a relative by marriage. The awards were handed over at the close by Mrs. Robertson Durham, Glencairn."

East Lothian Courier. September 1928

They also supported the Club in other ways. Mrs. Charlotte Thomson and Mrs. Emily Dryborough met in the Clubhouse every day at lunchtime for gin & tonics until their lunch was ready.

Fiona Anderson
1954–

Photo courtesy of SLGA

Fiona originally came from Blairgowrie but has been a member of GLGC since 1981. She won the Scottish Ladies' Championship in 1987 and was runner up in 1980, 83 and 88. Among her other wins were the North of Scotland Ladies' in 1977 and the Scottish Universities Champion in 1975.

Internationally, she played for Scotland thirteen times from 1977 to 1992. She also represented Britain in the Vagliano Trophy team in 1987 and was a member of the Curtis Cup squad in 1988.

Together with Catriona Matthew she won the Scottish Foursomes for three years consecutively in 1988, 89 and 90.

Lindsey Anderson
1965—

Lindsey joined Gullane in 1993 from Tain. She had been the most improved junior in the UK and won the 1st Golf Foundation Award. Internationally she played for Scottish Girls in 1982 and Scottish Schools in 1981 and 82. She played in the Under 21 European Team Championship in 1984 and 1986. At senior level, she represented Scotland seven times between 1987 and 1995, playing in the Home Internationals and the European Team Championship.

She was runner up in the Scottish Ladies' Championship in 1989 and won the Northern Counties Championship in 1994. Since joining GLGC she has dominated the Club Championship winning five times between 1994 and 2002. Lindsey was Captain of the Girls' International team in 2002 and 2003.

Kathleen Copley
nee Lackie
1943—

Kathleen was runner up in the Scottish Ladies' Championship in 1974 and represented Scotland in 1974 and 75. She went on to become Chairman of the SLGA in 1990. She became a member of GLGC in 1984.

Photo courtesy of SLGA

Millicent Couper
1902—1971

Millicent Couper won the Scottish Ladies' Championship in 1933 at Turnberry. She was a Scottish Internationalist six times between 1929 and 1938. She also played in 1956, having been beaten in the final of the Scottish Ladies' Championship at North Berwick by Jessie Valentine in 1955. Perhaps because of her own experiences she donated two cups in 1967 for the semi–finalists in the Scottish Championship. She played for Great Britain against France in 1935.

Photo courtesy of SLGA

She served on the Committee at GLGC from 1931 — 1934 and was proposed as Captain in 1933. She was one of the candidates at the AGM in the only contested election for Captain at GLGC when Mrs Wallace Williamson was elected. Her nickname, "Brasso", stuck after once being asked how she had got on in a match she had just played she replied "I polished them off!"

Golf was not her only interest as she was very involved in the life of North Berwick. She was a member of the Town Council for thirty years and of the County Council of East Lothian for twenty five years. She was the first woman to be appointed Provost of North Berwick from 1965 -68. In July 1968 the Freedom of the Burgh was conferred on her making her a Burgess of the Royal Burgh of North Berwick.

Mary Duncan
nee Wood
1898—1959

Although the exact date of Miss Mary Wood joining GLGC is not clear she was elected to the Committee in 1923 and became Captain in 1927. She won the Scottish Ladies' Championship in 1926.

She played for Scotland in 1925, 27, 28 and 1939. She was Midlothian Ladies' Champion in 1924, 25 and 26.

After she married she won the Championship of India in 1929 and 30. She returned to Scotland during the thirties and was elected back on to the Committee in 1938.

Mary Wood on winning the Scottish Ladies' Championship in 1926
Photo courtesy of SLGA

Marjory Ferguson
nee Fowler
1937—2003

Marjory made an enormous contribution to golf over the years both as a player and as an administrator. The Girls' Championship, now known as the Girls' British Amateur Golf Championship, was revived after the War by the LGU and Marjory was one of the promising youngsters, along with Connie Lugton and Ethel Jack , to play in the 1955 team.

Marjory Ferguson at the Scottish Ladies' Championship in 1966
Photo courtesy of SLGA

"As youngsters we always used to feel very honoured if we were asked to play with Mrs. Beddows or other Gullane luminaries such as Marjorie Draper and Jean Anderson. We did not get the coaching that young players receive today and we saw games with these great players as a vital part of our golfing education"

She was runner up in the Scottish Ladies' Championship in 1966 and 1971 and won the Portuguese Championship in 1970. She played in the Curtis Cup in 1966, three times in the European Team Championships and for the Vagliano Trophy team in 1965.

She won the East of Scotland Championship four times, in 1959–60–62–75. Together with Connie Lugton, she dominated the East Lothian Championship between 1957 and 1990. Marjory won fifteen times, the last time being in 1985 and Connie eleven times. Her name appears almost as frequently on the Championship Shield at GLGC—she won thirteen times between 1959 and 1985.

She joined GLGC in 1956 and was Captain of GLGC from 1981–82. Marjory was very involved with administration of Scottish Ladies' golf becoming Chairman of Scottish Girls from 1980—88, Chairman of the SLGA in 2000 and was Secretary of the East of Scotland Girls Golfing Association at the time of her death.

Ethel Jack
nee Philip
1939—

Ethel Jack joined GLGC in 1957 and became one of the three most promising girls at GLGC at that time -Connie Lugton, Marjory Fowler and Ethel. Her international golfing career has spanned all stages of her life. She played in the Scottish Girls' team in 1955 and played for Great Britain and Ireland against France in the Under 21 team. As a senior she played for Scotland in 1965, 66 and 67 and has also represented Scotland in the Vets team. During all this time, Ethel, who was a member of Prestonfield Golf Club also, was an indispensable member of the Midlothian County team.

As well as her golfing skill Ethel proved to have considerable leadership ability. This has perhaps been due in part to her irrepressible sense of fun. When Ethel is involved occasions are not allowed to become too formal and staid!

She was Secretary of Scottish Girls' Golf and served on the Executive Committee of the SLGA becoming Chairman from 1979 -81. She has been Captain of numerous teams and Clubs including Captain of GLGC from 1997 -98, Midlothian County Ladies from 1970–72, and Scottish Vets in 1995. She is a Past President of Midlothian County Ladies' Golf Club and President of the Scottish Veterans' Golfing Association. She also is the Scottish representative on the LGU Standard Scratch Score Committee.

Lesley Johnston
nee Hope
1955—

Lesley was brought up in Gullane having her first golf club in her hand at the age of three years. She became a member of GLGC in 1971.

The most memorable years of her golfing career were in the late seventies. Lesley won the Scottish Ladies' Championship in 1975 at Elie when she was only 20 and was the youngest winner for 64 years. She was runner up in 1979 at Gullane and in 1986 at St Andrews. She won the East of Scotland Ladies' Championship in 1977 and 1978. She represented Scotland eight times between 1975 and 1988 and was a member of several Scottish European Teams.

One of her great delights was being Captain of the Scottish team in 1988, 89 and 90—especially 1990 when Scotland were Champions. She has many happy memories of her international career.

"Whilst captaining a Scottish Under 21 team on our way to play at El Saler in Barcelona we bumped into Seve Ballesteros, one of my heroes, at Heathrow airport pushing his own luggage and clubs. He was extremely obliging and gave all of us his autograph which I still have today.

Lesley Johnston 2003

Although she now lives in Aberdeen she still regularly comes down to play in the medals and meetings of GLGC.

Gillian Kirkwood
1949 -

Gillian Kirkwood has been and is very involved in the administration and computerisation of Scottish Ladies' golf. She lives in Gullane and joined GLGC in 1995. She took over from Connie Lugton in 2002 as Membership Secretary and finds her computer skills are invaluable in keeping track of the members and candidates.

She was Ladies' Captain of Broomieknowe Golf Club in 1982–84 and is currently Vice Captain. The plan is that she will be Ladies' Captain again for their centenary year from 2005 -06. She was Captain of Midlothian Ladies' from 1990-92. After that she was appointed to the SLGA Executive in 1995 and became Chairman of SLGA in 2000. Perhaps because she has three daughters herself, all golfers, she has always been interested in junior golf. This has resulted in her becoming Chairman of the East of Scotland Girls from 2002. She has also qualified to become an official referee at golf championships by passing the R & A Rules of Golf tests.

During her time with SLGA she helped to design and implement their database and has developed her own database on the internet which gives information on the happenings, past and present, of Scottish Ladies' Amateur Golf as well as that of juniors and students. She is chairman of Midlothian Centenary Committee.

She, together with her husband, David Kirkwood, has developed a deep interest in the history of Ladies' Golf. This has led to her becoming a trustee of the British Women's Golf Museum. The history of Ladies' Golf also features on her database.

Barbara McIntosh
nee Dixon
1946—

Although Barbara's international career was in England before she joined GLGC she has been a dominant player at the Club and in East Lothian since her marriage in 1970. It has always been a matter of regret to her that, as an Englishwoman, she could not play in the main Scottish events.

Barbara was English Ladies' Champion in 1969 and represented England in 1969 and 1970. She was a member of the Vagliano Cup team in 1969, a Curtis Cup team reserve in 1970 and played in the European Team Championship for England in 1969. She was Dorset Champion three times in 1966, 68 and 70.

She won the East Lothian Championship in 1975 - the only person to do so apart from Marjory Ferguson and Connie Lugton between 1957 and 1981! She has been Club Champion three times -1981, 83 and 2000. She joined Gullane Ladies' Golf Club in 1970 and became Handicap Secretary from 1982–89. She won the Evening News Scottish Club Foursomes with Mrs Marjory Ferguson in 1971. In 1988 she became the Scottish Councillor to the LGU.

Barbara married into the Robertson Durham family circle with all its associations with GLGC as detailed earlier.

Gill Morrison
nee Cheetham
1942—

Gill was an English Girl Internationalist in 1960 and a finalist in the English Championship in 1965. She played for England in 1965 and also represented Great Britain in the Vagliano Trophy Team. She captained England in 1969 and 70. She joined GLGC after her marriage in 1970. Although renowned as indefatigable, latterly her golf has taken second place to the work she does for Riding for the Disabled and in keeping her livery stables functioning smoothly.

Lesley Nicholson
1976—

Lesley started playing at Haddington and joined GLGC as a junior in 1991. She won the Scottish Girls' Amateur Championship in 1994, the Scottish Ladies' Junior Open Stroke play Championship in 1999 and the Helen Holm Scottish Open Stroke play Championship in 1999. She won the Mackie Bowl in 1995 and the St Rule Trophy in 1999.

She played for Great Britain and Ireland in the Vagliano Trophy in 1999 and was a member of the Curtis Cup team in 2000. Internationally she played for Scottish Junior Girls in 1991–1994 and for Scotland from 1994–1999. Lesley turned professional in 2000.

Mrs W.H. Nicholson
nee Anderson

Mrs Nicholson in 1923
Photo courtesy of SLGA

Miss Anderson was the winner of the first competition run by GLGC—the Spring Meeting in May 1905. Having married in the summer she went on to win the first Autumn Meeting the same year in a play off with Miss Lugton as detailed in a later chapter.

Her name comes to the forefront when she won the Scottish Ladies' Championship in 1923 beating Mrs J.B. Watson, who had won three times consecutively, in the final at Lossiemouth. She represented Scotland in 1910, 1913 and 1925.

When Miss Wise resigned from the Club during the first World War, Mrs Nicholson took over and was Captain of GLGC from January 1918 through 1919.

The Parks
Doris Porter (1900 - 87) and Catherine Ritchie (1907 - 1987)

The Parks are a famous golfing family who were associated with Musselburgh for over 400 years. Willie Park won the Open Championship in the first year of its institution–1860– as well as in 1863,1866 and 1875. His brother Mungo won it in 1874. The third generation of this golfing family sustained a prominent golf association in Doris Porter, grand daughter of Willie Park and Catherine Ritchie, her cousin, both of whom were members of GLGC.

Doris Porter won the Scottish Ladies' Championship in 1936 and was runner up in 1929–30–31. She won the Midlothian Ladies' Championship five times consecutively from 1928 and the East of Scotland Championship in 1933 being runner up in 1931–38. She was runner up in the British Ladies' Championship in 1937 having been semi finalist in 1929 and 1933.

She played in the Curtis Cup in 1932, for Britain v. France in 1932–33–38 and for Scotland in the Home internationals thirteen times between 1922 and 1938.

Doris Park in 1936
Photo courtesy of SLGA

Katie Ritchie joined GLGC in 1932 and was elected to the Committee in 1933. She was Captain of the Club in 1963–64. She took over from her cousin in winning the Midlothian Ladies' Championship eleven times between 1933 and 1958. Runner up in the Scottish Ladies' Championship in 1938 and a semi finalist in 1947–48–58, she represented Scotland in the Home internationals six times between 1939 and 1953.

Mrs Catherine Ritchie

"In the final of the East of Scotland Women's Golf Championship, which was contested over Gullane No.1 yesterday by two members of Musselburgh's most famous golf family, Miss Doris Park defeated her cousin, Miss Cathie M. Park , in an exciting finish by a single hole.

Miss Doris Park is the better known of the two finalists. Miss Doris Park's father was Willie Park, an Open Champion and a great putter, and Miss Cathie Park is the daughter of his brother, Mungo Park. It is an interesting fact that Mrs Mungo Park won the Veteran Ladies' championship in the South two years ago."
East Lothian Courier 1933

Gertrude Percy,
nee Mitchell
1889— 1967

Mrs. Percy won the Scottish Ladies' Championship at Gullane in 1925 and, although not a member of Gullane at that time, joined shortly afterwards. She played most of her golf at Alnmouth in Northumberland and was Northumberland County Champion ten times between 1925 and 1938. She was a Scottish Internationalist in 1926,27, 28 and 31.

Miss Enid Wilson, in her book, A Gallery of Women Golfers, recounts how Mrs. Percy was in such deadly form on the greens at Gullane when winning her title there that the Post Office delivered straight to her a card addressed: "One Putt, Gullane". It stuck and after that she was referred to in golfing circles more frequently as "One Putt" than by her surname.

In 1938 she wished to become a non playing member of GLGC and although this was agreed it was pointed out that she could not then enter the Scottish Championship from Gullane and could not represent Gullane in the Eglinton Quaich. She changed her mind but in 1940 she did become a non playing member then resigned from GLGC in 1942.

Margaret Pickard
nee Nichol
1938—

Margaret was English Ladies' Champion in 1960 and runner up in 1957 and 67. She played in the Curtis Cup team in 1968 and in 1970; the Vagliano Cup team in 1959, 1961 and 1967. She represented England from 1957 until 1961 and then in 1967 and 1969.

"One of my most memorable events was playing as English Champion in the Home Internationals at Gullane in 1960. Knowing and loving the course must have helped me that week as I won five and a half points out of six!"

Margaret Pickard 2003

Between 1956 and 1982 Margaret won the Northumberland Ladies' County Championship fifteen times, a record number since its institution in 1921 . She won the Northern Ladies' Championship in 1957 and 58. She is rightly proud of the fact that she played for Northumberland from 1956 until 1988—thirty three consecutive years. As she herself said she somehow managed to fit in three children amongst that lot! All winter babies!

Margaret has always felt that the Gullane area was her second home from childhood days. She learned to play golf on the Children's Course at North Berwick and played in children's competitions in the summer holidays. She joined GLGC in 1962. Her mother, Mrs Nichol, was a well known member of the Club. Margaret's two daughters are carrying on the tradition and are also both members.

Anne Sime
1932—

Anne Sime joined GLGC in 1974 and became the Handicap Secretary from 1980–82 and Honorary Secretary from 1982 -89. She was Captain of East Lothian County Ladies' Golfing Association from 1989–90, Vice President from 2000–2003 and President from 2003. From 1991 she was a member of the SLGA Executive and rose to become Chairman from 1994–1995.

Anne wanted to encourage the higher handicap players in East Lothian and inaugurated the Sime Salver which is a Medal Foursomes tournament for East Lothian Clubs in 1990.

Jayne Smith
nee Ford
1967 –

Jayne was brought up in Gullane and joined the Club as a junior in 1980. She won the Scottish Ladies' Championship in 1999, represented Scotland in the Home Internationals in 1993–94–95–99 and was East Lothian Ladies' Champion in 1987, 2001and 2003. She was Scottish Schoolgirls' Champion in 1985. In 1999 she was a member of the Scottish Team for the European Ladies' Team Championship in Paris.

"I have always found it amusing just how difficult it is to win the Gullane Ladies' Club Championship. To the point that I won the Scottish Championship before I won my own Club Championship (it's that competitive). I had

been a member for ninteteen years before I finally managed it in 1999. I think it is great to play in a Club that has so many low handicap women competing, and I think that over the years it has done my golf good to be a small fish in a big pond!"

Jayne Smith 2003

Club Competition in 2003

Maureen Woodward driving off.

Photograph by Joyce Murdoch

CLUB COMPETITIONS AND MATCHES

Medal Competitions

The first competition held by the newly formed Club was the Spring Meeting over the Old Course in May 1905. The reports in The East Lothian Courier of the earliest competitions were detailed.

"In favourable golfing weather the members of Gullane Ladies' Club held their first annual spring meeting over the Old Course on Tuesday. Amongst the earlier actual returns was the very creditable figure of 89 by Miss Anderson, Edinburgh. ... Miss L. Lugton, one of the strongest of the lady players at Gullane, handed in a card only a stroke worse. ..Mrs Cotton, Edinburgh succeeded in carrying off the principal handicap award."

East Lothian Courier. 5th May 1905

"The members of the Gullane Ladies' Club held their annual Autumn meeting over the old course here on Tuesday. This was the second competition of the club, ...A very strong north easterly wind was blowing over the course and considerably affected the play, and, under the circumstances the score of 89 at which Mrs W.H. Nicholson, (nee Anderson) and Miss Lugton tied for scratch awards represented a most creditable performance."

East Lothian Courier 1st September 1905

As there was a tie for the scratch winner a play off was arranged.

" On Wednesday evening the tie for the scratch award was decided over the old course in a fairly stiff northerly breeze. Outward Miss Lugton played steady golf and turned at 46; but Mrs Nicholson was in quite irresistable form and completed the opening nine holes in the remarkable figure, for a lady, of 40.......Mrs Nicholson finished with a card of 81. As a result of her unusually fine performance, Mrs Nicholson was an easy winner of the scratch award. Miss Lugton..finished in 89."

East Lothian Courier 1st September 1905

Three medal competitions were held in 1906. In 1907 the Club decided to increase the number of medal competitions to six to be held from April to September on the last Tuesday of the month. The courses at Gullane were redesigned in 1909 and a third course was opened in 1910, the courses to be called No.1, originally "The Old Course", No.2, which was "The New Course" and No.3. In spite of many attempts to decide on more imaginative titles for these three beautiful courses these numbers have remained as their names. After the agreement with GGC in 1911 the Club decided to play April and September medals on No. 1, May and July on No. 2, and June and August on No. 3. At the same time the Club decided to change the day of the medal to the last Wednesday in the month; and so it remains to this day.

This format of competitions lasted, with a break for the First World War, until 1929 when Spring and Autumn Medal competitions were played as well as the six monthly medals. This number of monthly medals was increased to twelve the following year on the recommendation of the LGU.

The habit of playing a tie for the scratch prize in the event of two or more players having the same scratch score in a medal was discontinued in 1932 and the scratch prize decided on the last nine holes. There was some dispute about the details of this but the LGU decreed that "it is usual for ties to be settled on the last 9,6 or 3 holes with half, third or sixth handicap deducted".

In 1933 players were divided into Silver and Bronze sections depending on their handicaps. At the Spring and Autumn Meetings there were Silver and Bronze Handicap Divisions with prizes in each division. The sweep money at monthly medals was divided between the two handicap divisions. At that time there were scratch and handicap prizes irrespective of division.

Over the years these decisions have stood the test of time with some small alterations. Two additional medals are played in June and October. Because of the large number of members now playing in medals, Silver and Bronze handicap members play on different courses in some months. In 1969, in a move to accommodate members who worked during the week, alternate days for medals were accepted. Partners for the Spring, Summer and Autumn Meetings have been drawn from 1971 onwards.

Club Championship

After the Second World War golf at GLGC took on a vigorous lease of life. A Club Championship knockout was played in 1947 with Mrs. Beddows being the first winner of the magnificent Stiles Trophy. By 1981 few people were entering the Championship so the format was changed; the sixteen members with the best scores in the Spring Meeting qualified. As the Club Championship was necessarily restricted to low handicap players a Bronze Championship began in 1983 for the first sixteen Bronze players in the Spring Meeting. At present the qualifying competition is the May Medal.

Singles Competitions

The first Ladies Singles' Competition took place in September 1904 arranged by Mr. Richard Watson of GGC. In 1905 there were forty entrants - visiting and resident. Miss R.M. Watson, a member of GLGC, won it. GLGC took over the running of the competition in 1911 but it was suspended at the start of the First World War.

Bogey competitions were popular in both singles and foursomes format. A singles Bogey competition was held in May each year.

"The members of Gullane Ladies' Club held their annual Bogey competition over the No. 2 course at Gullane in fine weather. A stiff westerly breeze made the task set the lady golfers to defeat the "Colonel" – invariably a redoubtable opponent—all the more difficult, and, although he was unbeaten over the day's play, one competitor halved the match, and quite a number of others succumbed only by a narrow margin"

East Lothian Courier. May 1924

The Challenge Bowl Hole and Hole Tournament was started in 1921 and continues to this day. Originally a tie was decided by playing three holes. In 1937 this was changed to one hole. From 1971 rounds have been played one round per month from April to September.

Foursomes Competitions

From the beginning of the Club, Bogey Foursomes had always been played on No 3 in the afternoons after the Spring and Autumn Meetings. In 1950 it was decided that members could play in the Bogey Foursomes even if they had not played in the medal round in the morning. Eventually, in 1960, the Bogey Foursomes were played on a different day from the Spring and Autumn Meeting. Perhaps the members were getting older and two rounds in one day were too much! Partners were drawn until 1964 after which members chose their own partners. A further change in 1984 meant that these foursomes changed from Bogey to Stableford Foursomes and are now played as the Bi–Annual Foursomes in April and September.

Jubilee Foursomes were played in 1935 to coincide with the Royal visit in July. This was a knock out tournament played over No. 2. Eventually the ties were spread from April to September and, because of difficulty in arranging matches on No. 2, were played over No. 1 from 1972 onwards.

In 1949 two 36 hole Foursomes Medals were played in May and October, with high and low handicap players drawn together. With so many other fixtures now on the list this has been reduced to one 18 hole Foursome Medal played in May.

In 1950, the Winter Foursomes (knock out) competition was started. It was played between October to March. Partners were drawn until 1962 after which members chose their own partners.

Invitation Foursomes

The Invitation Foursomes were started in 1971 with members able to invite a player from another club to play in a Stableford competition. These continue, combining with the Charity Open Foursomes every second year, since 2000 .

Charity Day

A feature of Gullane is the Charity Open Day. The first Charity Day was in 1978 under the captaincy of Mrs. Catherine Robertson Durham. The charity chosen was Action Research for the Crippled Child. The committee decided to have a tombola, a cake and candy stall and a plant stall which were to be situated in the Ladies' Lounge.

The members were very distressed and shaken by Jean Anderson's very sudden death in 1984 and decided to have an Open Charity Tournament in 1985 in aid of The Jean Donald Memorial Fund used for multiple sclerosis sufferers at Leuchie, a charity close to Jean Anderson's heart. This competition was particularly successful. Entries came from all over Britain, many excellent prizes were donated and Mrs Jessie Valentine agreed to present the prizes. The members raised over £4000.

Gullane Charity Day in 1998

Back LtoR: Clare Howarth, Shona Low, Elaine Carnie, Carol Henderson, Joanne Watt, Nan Cook
Front: Margaret Milligan, Jane Miller, Ethel Jack (Captain), Representative of Friends of Sick Kids, Vickie Sandeman, Morag Younie

From 1988 a Charity Open Day has been held every two years with the current Captain able to choose which Charity should benefit. There is usually a tombola, a raffle, a plant and produce stall as well as various competitions such as 'Name the doll', devised by enterprising members. The competition started as a Medal round but has evolved into an Open Foursomes Stableford competition.

The Charities which have benefited over the years together with the Captain of the day are:

1978	Action Research for the Crippled Child	Mrs Robertson Durham
1985	Jean Anderson Memorial Fund	Mrs McLean Ross
1988	St Columba's Hospice	Mrs McLeod
1990	Chest, Heart and Stroke	Mrs Anne Jack
1992	Fairmile Nursing Home	Mrs Tait
1994	Oncology Department , Western General	Mrs Matthews
1996	Macmillan Nurses	Miss Lugton
1998	Friends of Sick Children's Hospital	Mrs Ethel Jack
2000	Royal Blind School	Mrs Carnie
2002	Children's Hospice	Mrs Sneddon

Mixed Competitions

Mixed golf has always been popular at Gullane.

"A tournament in mixed doubles, under handicap conditions, was concluded at Gullane, the play extending over several days. The contest which was promoted by Mr R.M. Watson proved very popular, seventy two competitors taking part."

East Lothian Courier May 1905

Gullane Golf Club continued to organise a Mixed Doubles tournament annually in September until 1932 when GLGC offered to help GGC run it. This has evolved into the Mixed Stableford Competition held at the beginning of June.

At present there are an increasing number of mixed competitions: Mixed Invitation Foursomes and Barbeque at the end of June, a Tri–Am with GGC at the end of July and a Shotgun Mixed Foursomes in August.

The Hankey Pankey

In 1981 a trophy called the Hankey Pankey Trophy was found in the Clubhouse in a cupboard under the stairs. This was a trophy from a group of players calling themselves the Hankey - Pankeys which originated in 1871. Membership of this society was restricted as John Kerr explains in his book.

"It was a certificate of character for no–one was asked, who sat by the wayside of life clad in sackcloth and ashes, and looked on life's enjoyments with eyes which had been steeped in the juice of the lemon"

John Kerr. The Golf Book of East Lothian 1897

Mr Iain Cowan, Captain of GGC, approached Marjory Ferguson, Captain of GLGC, and suggested a Mixed Foursomes knockout competition played over the summer months. A Consolation Stableford mixed foursomes competition is played on the day of the final of the knockout competition with the consolation trophy presented by Mr Cowan and Mrs Ferguson. Both these competitions are well supported but it is not recorded if those taking part all conform to John Kerr's description.

Mackie Bowl

In 1974 Connie Lugton, Ethel Jack, Marjory Ferguson and other members at the Club felt that it was time that GLGC should have an Open tournament for low handicap players both for the benefit of Scottish Ladies' golf and also to enable them to return the hospitality they were granted at other tournaments in Scotland such as the Helen Holm trophy at Troon. The Gullane Ladies' Open was played for the first time in 1974 but there was no trophy. In 1975 Mrs. Elsie Mackie presented a beautiful trophy, a Monteith bowl. The competition was then renamed the Mackie Bowl and has been played for annually ever since.

Mrs Maureen Matthews, Mrs Elsie Mackie, Miss Connie Lugton with the Mackie Bowl

Photograph courtesy of Mrs Maureen Matthews

GLGC members have figured among the winners:

1977	Miss Lesley Hope
1980	Miss Fiona Anderson
1986	Miss Lesley Hope
1987	Miss Fiona Anderson
1989	Mrs Marjory Ferguson
1995	Miss Lesley Nicholson

In 1996, Janice Moodie set the course record with 67 over No. 1

MATCHES

One of the objectives of the founders of GLGC was to play matches against other Clubs. The first match played by Gullane Ladies was against Murrayfield Ladies in May 1905.

"Twelve players a–side met in a match over the Old Course at Gullane in favourable weather. The play was by singles and the games were counted on the points system. The Gullane Ladies won by a majority of five matches."

East Lothian Courier May 1905

However, Gullane was not so successful in the return match in June 1905 when Murrayfield won by 8 matches to 1. After this start matches do not feature in the minutes of the club until 1931 when a match against Longniddry was arranged. From then on matches against Alnmouth, Murrayfield and Longniddry were regularly arranged although apparently not every year. Nowadays regular annual matches are organised against the other East Lothian Clubs with teams drawn from a range of the members. They are held in a great spirit of friendliness and provide a good opportunity for golfers to meet each other and to play on each others courses.

The McIntosh Quaich

In 1949 a match against Dirleton Castle was proposed. This has become an annual event in the Club and the McIntosh Quaich is eagerly contested.

The Bowhill Cup

After the war a foursomes match of GLGC members against GGC members was proposed and has come to be known as The Bowhill Cup. It is fiercely contested each year with the best players at GLGC being asked to play for the trophy presented by Mr & Mrs Ian Bowhill.

NATIONAL TEAM COMPETITIONS

Gullane has had a tradition of entering teams for national team championships[5]. Among the best known are the Eglinton Quaich, The Grainger Cup, Daily Mail Foursomes and the Scottish Ladies Foursomes. As can be seen from Appendix 5 the teams have had many successes in the past although recently there has been intense competition from other Clubs and GLGC does not feature so frequently among the winners.

Eglinton Quaich winning team in 1925.

L to R: Miss Marjory Thomas, Miss Doris Park, Miss Mary Wood, Mrs Wallace Williamson.

Competitors at the Bowhill Cup
May 2003

Trophy Cabinet in Ladies' lounge.

Photograph by Joyce Murdoch

PRIZES AND TROPHIES

Prizes and Trophies for Medal winners

If the members of GLGC read about the prizes which were awarded to the Medal winners in1905 they might feel they are golfing in the wrong era!

"..the scratch award was a golf pendant along with which went a prize in kind. The principal handicap award was a gold bracelet, with accompanying pendant, the bracelet to become the property of the player winning it thrice, and not necessarily in succession. Two club allowance prizes in kind were also offered."

East Lothian Courier May 1905

The magnificent prizes on this occasion were presented by Mrs R.M.Watson and thus began the tradition at GLGC whereby many members have generously donated beautiful trophies.

Over the years the prizes presented at each of the Medal competitions has been the subject of much debate; they have slowly increased from 10/- vouchers in 1906 to £10 in 2002 for the scratch and handicap winners of the medals. These vouchers have been a matter of concern in the past.

"Some of the prize winners are spending their money on silk stockings, fur lined gloves etc. and would it not be better to give prizes of balls to get away from this difficulty"

GLGC Minutes, 1923

As the Amateur Status Committee of the Royal and Ancient Club would not have approved these purchases it was decided that vouchers should only be valid at the local golf shop. This is still the case.

From 1929 there was a sweepstake at each medal. There has been much discussion about which winners win what in each medal. Vouchers are given to the scratch winner and the first three handicap winners in the silver section and to the first four handicap winners in the bronze section. This only changes if the bronze division is playing on a different course from the silver medal when there is also a scratch prize for the bronze players. The sweep is divided amongst the handicap winners.

Scratch Bowl

After the initial flurry of magnificent prizes for scratch players in 1905, the Club decided in 1907 to give just one scratch medal to be presented yearly. Even this was stopped in 1909 when there was no scratch medal but a prize of 15/-. In 1913 the scratch winner of each medal won a teaspoon.

In 1923 Mrs Rome presented a Scratch Bowl to be won outright by the player whose name appeared most on the trophy after three years. Miss M. J. Wood won it outright in 1925. Lord Derby donated a replacement trophy but it was decided that this should not be won outright but presented biannually. The player with the best scratch score in the Spring and Autumn meetings wins the bowl.

Bronze Scratch Salver

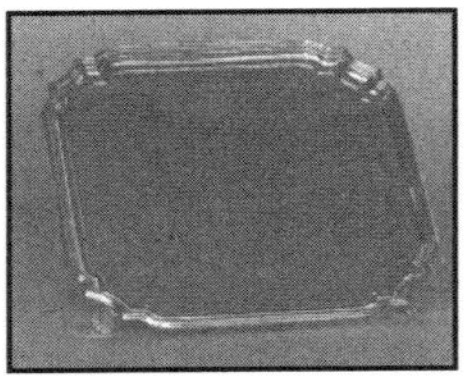

In 1970 Mrs Draper presented a silver salver for the player in the bronze division with the best scratch score in the Spring and Autumn meetings.

Handicap Quaich

Miss Law donated a trophy in 1906 to be won by the member with the best aggregate of three net scores from the six medals played. After three seasons the most frequent winner was to have possession of the cup. Miss M.Alloway won the trophy in 1909, Miss Robertson Durham won the replacement in 1912 and Miss Stiles won the next replacement, donated by Lord Dunedin, Captain of GGC, in 1915. Competitions were then suspended for the First World War and it was not until 1921 that the trophy was replaced. This new trophy was won by Mrs R.O. Pitman in 1925.

Perhaps the Club was becoming aware of the cost of continually replacing trophies. When Mrs Hall Blyth presented a quaich in 1926 it was decided that it would not be won outright in future but presented biannually every year to the member with the best handicap score in the Spring and Autumn meetings.

Bronze Handicap Bowl

In 1933 players were divided into Silver and Bronze depending on their handicap. Mrs Turnbull presented a silver bowl in 1934 for the member in the bronze division with the best handicap score in the Spring and Autumn meetings.

Jean Donald Trophy

In 1952 Jean Donald gave a silver cigarette box for the best handicap aggregate at the Spring and Autumn meetings.

Leeds Quaich

Dr Leeds, while Captain of Gullane Golf Club in 1984, presented a quaich for the player in the bronze division with the best aggregate at the Spring and Autumn meetings.

The Beddows Cup

Mr Steel, Charlotte Beddows' nephew, donated a cup in her memory in 1977. Initially it was presented to the winners of an eclectic foursomes competition in October but latterly has been won by the player with the best handicap score in the Summer meeting.

The Mann Trophy

Mr & Mrs Mann, stewards at the Club, presented a decanter when they left to go to New Zealand in 1994 to thank the Ladies for their support. It is awarded to the player with the best handicap score in the March medal.

Woozie Grant Trophy

When Ursula Grant died while Vice Captain in 1996 her family presented a trophy to be won by the player with the best aggregate in the two stableford medals in June and October.

Menzies Trophy

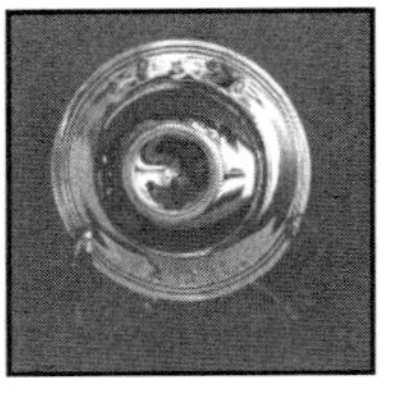

In 1978 Mrs Menzies presented a silver dish to be won by the player reducing her handicap from 36 by the greatest number of strokes. As this trophy was not presented in 1981 the scope was widened to include players with handicaps between 30-36. This was modified again and is now awarded to the player in handicap category 5 or 6 who has returned the net score most below par in LGU competitions.

Trophies for Other Competitions

Stiles Trophy

Lady Stiles and her daughter, Mrs Rome, presented the Stiles Trophy, a copy of a bowl taken from Traprain, in memory of Sir Harold Stiles. This is awarded to the winner of the Club Championship which started in 1947.

Bronze Championship Bowl

Mrs McLean Ross and Mrs Antonio, Captains from 1983-1986 presented, a silver bowl for the winner of the Bronze Championship.

Jubilee Cup

Sir Alfred Bingham presented a silver cup in 1935 for the winners of the Jubilee Foursomes, the knock out Summer Foursomes competition.

Challenge Bowl

Gullane Golf Club donated the Challenge Bowl in 1921 for the winner of the annual handicap knockout tournament known as the Challenge Bowl Hole and Hole tournament.

Watson Salvers

Mrs Beddows presented two silver salvers for the winners of the Club Bogey Foursomes played after the Spring and Autumn meetings, now the Bi Annual Foursomes played in April and September.

Medal Foursomes Cups

Two silver miniature cups are presented to the winners of the Medal Foursomes in May

Winter Foursomes

Two bon bon dishes were presented by Mrs G.W. Miller in 1954 for the winners of the Winter Foursomes knock out competition.

Carlyle Shield

A Round Robin competition was begun in 1984 for higher handicap players. Mrs Elaine Carlyle presented the shield for the winner in 1985

Bowhill Cup

Mr & Mrs Ian Bowhill presented a cup in 1953 for the winners of the annual match, now called the Bowhill Cup, between GGC and GLGC.

McIntosh Quaich

The match between GLGC and Dirleton Castle started in 1949 and in 1952 Mrs Angela McIntosh presented the McIntosh Quaich for the winning club.

Mackie Bowl

Mrs Mackie presented a Monteith bowl in 1974 for the winner of the Ladies Open Singles tournament, now called the Mackie Bowl.

Junior Trophies

The junior members of the Club are valued and their achievements duly recognised. It appears from the minutes that the first trophy for younger members was a quaich, presented by Miss Kellie in 1957. It was not strictly for juniors as it was a junior aggregate handicap trophy for members under 25. There is no further reference to this trophy.

Crofthill Cup

This cup, presented by Mrs Elise Guy, is won by the Junior Champion.

Most Improved Junior

Mrs Matthews presented a rock crystal in 1993 for the junior who improved their handicap by the most strokes in the year.

Robin Brooch

A junior eclectic is played each year. Mrs Anne Jack presented a brooch for the winner.

Junior Open

Gullane Golf Club started a Junior Open for boys and girls in 2001. Mrs Margaret Sneddon presented a trophy for the girl who had the best scratch score. GLGC presented a trophy for the girl who had the best handicap score.

GLGC Committee entertaining their guests at the Scottish Ladies' Championship in 1994

LtoR Back: Sheila Baird, Elaine Carnie, Kathleen Stormonth, Elspeth Marshall, Connie Lugton, Margaret McGregor, Lesley Gray, Judy Cuthbertson
Front : Maureen Woodward, Maureen Matthews
Photograph courtesy of Mrs Maureen Matthews

SOCIAL EVENTS

Just as the first members of 1905 would be astonished at the number and scope of the golfing events arranged nowadays each year at the Club so they would be amazed at the range of social activities arranged by the Committee.

In 1905 the main purpose of the Club and Clubhouse was to enable the Lady Members to play golf in an organized and comfortable way. Over the years the Club has entertained visiting players and others especially when attending Championships held at Gullane. The Clubhouse has also proved to be somewhere for the members to play bridge and, in the later years, to attend other social functions organized by the Committee.

Entertaining visitors

The only social event mentioned in the early minutes of the Club was when the Scottish Ladies' Championship was held at Gullane in 1908. The clubhouse at that time was Alex Aitken's "shed" in Saltcoats Road. The Ladies made their Clubhouse available for competitors and served teas in the nearby school. When the Championship was held at Gullane again in 1925 the Club had moved into Shepherd's Cottage. The Committee wanted to make the Clubhouse more comfortable for the competitors so comfortable chairs were brought downstairs to the kitchen where tea, coffee and bovril were to be served.

After the Ladies moved into the present Clubhouse there was much more scope for socialising and the Ladies made sure that their own bar was properly stocked with beer, cider, whisky, gin, French & Italian vermouth, port, sherry, brandy and sloe gin. The profit from the sale of the drink was handed over to GGC in exchange for service. There was little full catering but members bringing their own lunch and tea were requested not to eat it in the Clubhouse.

Come the fifties and the Ladies felt able to stretch their hospitable wings. In 1950 the Australian Ladies' Golf Team and their hostesses were invited for tea and drinks. Money was still very tight after the war so this was much appreciated by the LGU and the SLGA. In 1952 the Curtis Cup was played at Muirfield. GLGC invited the Curtis Cup teams and officials to a cocktail party in the Clubhouse. 1954 saw the 50th anniversary of the Club. This was celebrated by a cocktail party in the Clubhouse and a bench placed at the 6th tee on No 1.

It has now become a tradition that there should be a cocktail party when there is a major Ladies' or Girls' Championship or Match held at Gullane or Muirfield. This extended to a sandwich lunch for the Curtis Cup team in 1972. Competitors, officials and members alike seem to appreciate the hospitality very much. The Curtis Cup Saucer Match for past players and supporters was held at Gullane. The players presented a signed picture as a memento.

1982 was the centenary year of Gullane Golf Club and GLGC decided to present GGC with a Captain's badge. The badge was made up by James Ness & Son in Edinburgh who took a great deal of time and energy making sure that the badge, made in old gold, was exactly to specification. It was presented to Mr Evan Cuthbertson, Captain of GGC, at a cocktail party hosted by GLGC.

Picture presented by the competitors at the Saucer Match in 1972. This is in the Ladies' lounge

The Curtis Cup was held at Muirfield in 1984 and GLGC members continued the tradition of entertaining the visitors.

" In 1984 I had the great privilege of being invited to play a round of golf over No 1 course with Glenna Collett Vare. I was not aware at the time of this fine old lady's pedigree in the annals of Ladies' golf—US Amateur Champion, six times Canadian Champion, twice runner up in our British Championship and four Curtis Cup appearances, captaining the American side three times.

It was a wet and windy morning, but this redoubtable 81 year old would not even contemplate enjoying the comfort of the clubhouse instead of playing. After 18 holes we had a quick bite of lunch, then off to Edinburgh

to buy some gifts for the family at home. My day finished when I dropped her off at Greywalls, where she was staying as a guest of the LGU. There was just time for a quick shower and hairdo before the Curtis Cup dinner.

I enjoyed a wonderful day with a lady who, even at 81 years old, had a great skill but above all a wonderful sense of humour and appreciation of the game of golf."

Mrs Carol McLeod, Captain 1987-88

In 1994 the Scottish Ladies' Championship was held at Gullane. The Club decided to host an evening as they had always done in the past and the Committee were told they would have to do a "turn". They performed a song to the tune of "We belong tae Glasgow" (Appendix 7) .

"Because many people thought of the members of GLGC as being somewhat prim and ladylike one of the Committee, Mrs. Elaine Carnie, suggested we should look vampish! She also wrote a very funny song. When we appeared in the dining room the laughter and noise was tremendous. The young competitors were obviously taken by surprise."

Mrs Maureen Matthews, Captain 1993-94

This habit of entertaining was continued at the dinner for the European Boys Championship in 1998. GLGC had been asked to provide "hostesses" for each team of boys. At the final dinner the Committee decided to shed some of this matronly aspect and dressed up to perform a song and dance routine "Swinging in the Rain".

Photograph courtesy of Mrs Kay McLean Ross

Bridge in the Clubhouse

Since the 1920s bridge has been extremely popular with the members of GLGC. It has sometimes been difficult to reconcile the needs of the bridge players with those of the other members.

After World War I the members started playing bridge in the Clubhouse. This has continued over the years both for pleasure and for the purpose of raising money for charity. In 1940 an afternoon bridge party was held to raise money for the Duchess of Northumberland's Benevolent and Comforts Fund for the A.T.S. and raised the sum of £47. 2/6. Another bridge party was held in early 1941 in aid of the Golfers' Spitfire Fund. This raised £80.

The question of playing bridge in the clubhouse has often exercised the Committee. Many members were very enthusiastic bridge players and it is still a very popular activity. When the members played in the Ladies' lounge or Clubroom as it was called there was some times conflict between the "golfers" and "bridge players". In March 1947 the minutes record that

"Playing bridge in the Clubroom during the summer months was discussed. It was agreed that two tables should be put up permanently at the end of the room and that a notice should be put telling players that they must play at the tables as placed and that they must not expect silence."

GLGC Minutes March 1947

Eventually this problem receded as the Ladies were allowed to use the Card Room for bridge.

A bridge tournament and film show of the Championship in aid of the East Lothian Ladies' County Golf Association was held in November 1947. Men were permitted entry to the Ladies' Lounge on that date! Another bridge party was held in 1953 to raise money for the Village Council Coronation Fund. Bridge parties continue to be held regularly in the Clubhouse and are an excellent way of raising money for deserving causes.

Entertaining the members

After almost 75 years the members began entertaining themselves! Captain's Day, coffee mornings, dinners and buffet lunches have become regular features of GLGC life.

Captain's Day is held in April. In 1976 Mrs. Marguerite Roberts who was Captain at the time held a most successful Captain's Day to which all new members were invited with the purpose of introducing them to other members of the Club. This has continued with all members attending playing Medal Foursomes over 9 holes then tea in the Clubhouse. In 2003 a new format was tried ; 18 holes on No.3 with four starting points. This was followed by wine and canapes in the Clubhouse.

Coffee mornings held in the winter were officially started in 1977. The members seem to enjoy meeting for coffee and, weather permitting, playing a few holes during the winter months. From 1995 the format of some of the coffee mornings has changed with speakers or other events being organized for the morning and money raised for charity. There have been talks on oriental rugs, Antarctica, Madagascar, Nepal, Rachel House and talks by a physiotherapist and a colour consultant Events have included a slide show, a book sale and a scarf exchange.

During the winter "get togethers" have been played since 1985 on one morning during the week although not every year. The members play foursomes over 9 or 18 holes with drawn partners depending on the weather.

Mrs Marguerite Roberts realized that with so many members playing in the Autumn Meeting it was unrealistic to expect that members who played early in the morning would wait for the prize giving in the late afternoon. She suggested that the prize giving for the Autumn Meeting be held at the AGM instead of the traditional habit of holding it after the meeting. However this proved to be rather too much all at once and the Annual Autumn Prizegiving was combined with a Buffet Lunch instead of with the AGM in 1984. This was more satisfactory to the members and is now held annually in November.

The Spring Prize giving was traditionally held after the Spring meeting. As had happened at the Autumn Meeting fewer people were prepared to wait for the prize giving after they had played. It was then held in conjunction with a Buffet Lunch which was held in Spring from 1985 until 2001. In 2002 the Captain, Margaret Sneddon, decided to have a dinner and prize giving and then entertainment by some members.

In the early 80's there was concern that the Clubhouse was not being used enough. There has since been a flurry of social events in the Clubhouse. Mrs Tait, as Captain, revived evening functions in 1992 with a Fashion Show and an Antiques Road Show. Mrs Matthews built on this with several new functions: Mrs Given, an official with the LGU, spoke at a Rules of Golf evening in Spring1993; a foursomes match between a Captain's and a Secretary's team was held in July and has become an annual event; there was a food and a Christmas decoration demonstration evening; a Burns Supper which was held in January 1994 found a "wealth of talent" among the members and even included a solitary man, Mr Ian Cowan, who proposed the Toast to the Lassies! Since 1984 an unofficial competition was held on January 2nd; this has since become an official annual event. Subsequent Captains had their own ideas – St Andrews Night, a Summer supper and a drinks party at which games for the following day were arranged.

Spring Prizegiving May 2003

LtoR. Back: Wendy Lourie, Pat Fraser, Anne Jack, Doreen Donaldson, Susan Hume
Front: Clare Kirkwood, Elaine Carnie, Carrie Kirkwood

The Millenium

The Millenium saw extra celebrations at the Club. Mrs Elaine Carnie was Captain at the time and recalls the events of the year.

"For a start there are no useful Notes for Guidance. No Gullane Ladies' Golf Club existed at the last millenium so my trusty Committee and I set off down the avenue of the great unknown with trepidation.

A Millenium Steering Group was set up in conjunction with Gullane Golf Club. The first meeting took place in a pub in Edinburgh, and an hour later, as the ideas and claret flowed, we were in no doubt whatsoever that the year would be packed with innovative and memorable events, each quite unique, for no other reason than being prefaced by the word "Millenium".

The Millenium Festive Frenzy in January was snowed off but was saved by mulled wine and mince pies. In February the World Premiere of our millenium film: "A Day in the Life of Gullane Ladies' Golf Club" was shown to a packed coffee morning. This cameo production, expertly filmed, edited and narrated by Mrs Judy Spielberg– Cuthbertson, was to launch our charity year. This fund was substantially increased by various members paying Judy not to show the film again!

"Leap into the Millenium" was a new venture—a shotgun foursome. Any future Captain contemplating a repeat of this event should be aware that the 2000 decibel marine foghorn is not sufficient to attract the attention

of 144 ladies chatting on 18 different tees, and that some sort of desert crossing vehicle is necessary to ensure that ladies arrive at the 13th in time for the start. We all finally met up for an excellent lunch at dusk.

Millenium Captain's Day in April was not unlike any other Captain's Day except that, because of a slight numerical misunderstanding on my part I had ordered tea for 28 ladies instead of 56. The Committee leapt into action cutting scones in half, unwrapping emergency crockery and winging loaves from freezer to microwave. A floral display was snatched from the mantelpiece and presented to the steward. The assembled gathering seemed to think it was all incredibly amusing.

Millenium Ladies' Day in June raised £700 for Breast Cancer research by paying to play on our own course in exchange for a "goodie bag". We had a huge entry for this when it was discovered that the "goodie bag" included an anti-wrinkle treatment!

July now and excitement over the Millenium Ball was tangible. This was the first ever Ball held by the Clubs. Meetings took place over months with tent erectors, insurance brokers, caterers, wine suppliers, florists, bandleaders, photographers etc and finally, on 8th July everything fell into place. A brilliant evening was had by 300 members of both clubs.

The next day a Millenium Mixed Shotgun Foursome took place followed by a magnificent buffet in the marquee. All in all, a most memorable Millenium weekend."

Elaine Carnie, Captain 1999-2000

The 21st Century

At the start of 2001 the Captain, Mrs Margaret Sneddon, organized joint social events with GGC. A talk on the history of golf, a wine tasting, dinner and quiz, a Rules of Golf night and a St Andrew's Night dinner with in-house entertainment were all well attended by members of both Clubs. In August 2002 a Shot Gun Mixed Foursome with a draw for partners followed by lunch was a very sociable occasion and is now an annual fixture.

Members entertaining at a St Andrews Night dinner. LtoR: Catherine Ferguson , Pauline Scott, Grace Gilhooley, Margaret Sneddon, Lesley Gray

Photograph courtesy of Margaret Sneddon

Margaret Sneddon wanted to show Club support for international golf matches. She organised a bus outing to the Solheim Cup held at Loch Lomond and to the WPGA Championship at Turnberry in 2002. Both outings were well supported and gave GLGC members who went much fun as well as golf spectating. In fact Peter Alliss met Margaret and some of the other Ladies at the WPGA Championship and announced on television that they had been in such cracking form enjoying their Pimms that he wouldn't like to be in the bus on the way home as he thought it might be resounding to the sound of singing!

Centenary Celebrations

The main Centenary celebrations are to take place over the weekend of September 10th, 11th and 12th, 2004. There is a formal dinner at the Roxburgh Hotel on Friday 10th September. On Saturday there is to be a Stableford Competition over No.1 and on Sunday a Shotgun Foursomes over Nos 2 and 3. This will be a fun competition and the competitors are to dress in the golf fashions of some period between 1904 –2004. This will be followed by a cocktail party and prizegiving.

On December 1st 2004, the Captain and past Captains will gather for a lunch. To commemorate the inaugural meeting of GLGC, a toast will be made to the founder members of Gullane Ladies' Golf Club and to the next century of the Club.

APPENDIX 1

THE ORIGINAL MEMBERS ON 1ST DECEMBER 1904

Mrs Alloway
Miss Alloway
Mrs A. Mackenzie
Miss Effie Mackenzie
Miss Emma Mackenzie
Mrs Milligan
Miss Dowell
Miss E Dowell
Mrs Watson
Mrs A.M. Ross
Miss M Law
Mrs Caesar
Miss Cotton
Miss L. Lugton
Miss Watson
Miss M Aitchison
Mrs A.S. Ritchie
Miss Ross
Mrs W Ritchie
Miss M McIntosh
Miss C McIntosh
Miss Cairns
Mrs MacGregor
Lady Spearman
Miss S Spearman
Miss Sime
Miss M Alloway
Mrs Carphin
Miss Ewart
Mrs A J Lawrie
Miss May Lennox
Mrs Millar
Mrs Nicholson
Miss Candyside
Miss E H Cairns
Mrs L Mackenzie
Mrs Alexis Thomson
Miss Scott
Mrs Paul
Mrs Rayner
Mrs Gardiner
Mrs Goad
Mrs Wallace Williamson
Mrs Dunn
Mrs Sewill

APPENDIX 2

CAPTAINS OF GULLANE LADIES' GOLF CLUB

1905	Lady Spearman
1906	Mrs C.Cotton
1907	Miss M. Law
1908	Miss Dowell
1909	Mrs A.S.Ritchie
1910	Mrs Alloway
1911	Mrs G.Cotton
1912	Miss L. Lugton
1913	Miss M. Lennox
1914	Mrs A.W. Robertson Durham
1915	Mrs L.G. Thomas
1916-17-18	Miss E.A. Wise
1919	Mrs Nicholson
1920	Mrs Marshall
1921	Mrs R.W. Stevenson
1922	Miss M.H. Paul
1923	Mrs Murray Stuart
1924	Mrs W. Thomson
1925	Mrs B.Hall Blyth
1926	Mrs T. Dryborough
1927	Miss M.J.Wood
1928	Mrs R.O. Pitman
1929	Mrs S.G. Rome
1930	Mrs J.D.Dawson
1931	Mrs A.H. Bowhill
1932	Mrs P.Turnbull
1933	Mrs Leslie Brown
1934-35	MrsR.H. Wallace Williamson
1936-37	Miss M.M. Robertson Durham
1937-46	Mrs I.H. Bowhill
1947-48	Mrs S.G. Rome
1949-50	Mrs R.T. Peel
1951-52	Miss J. Donald
1953-54	Mrs J.D.H. McIntosh
1955-56	Mrs G.W.Mackie
1957-58	Mrs C.H. Hay
1959-60	Mrs D.F. Wishart
1961-62	Miss M. Druitt
1963-64	Mrs W.C. Ritchie
1965-66	Mrs A.L. McClure
1967-68	Miss E.C. McLarty
1969-70	Miss C.Corstorphine
1971-72	Mrs K. Hay Smith
1973-74	Miss G.A.D. Pearson
1975-76	Mrs S.M.Roberts
1977-78	Mrs G. Robertson Durham
1979-80	Mrs D.G. Andrew
1981-82	Mrs A.J.R. Ferguson
1983-84	Mrs J. McLean Ross
1985-86	Mrs D. Antonio
1987-88	Mrs H.McLeod
1989-90	Mrs R.R. Jack
1991-92	Mrs J. Tait
1993-94	Mrs M.R.A. Matthews
1995-96	Miss C.J. Lugton
1997-98	Mrs P.G. Jack
1999-00	Mrs E.C. Carnie
2001-02	Mrs M. N. Sneddon
2003-04	Mrs J. Cuthbertson

APPENDIX 3

OFFICIALS OF THE CLUB

Secretaries of Gullane Ladies' Golf Club

1904 - 1913	Mrs R. M. Watson
1913 - 1918	Miss D. Stiles became Mrs Rome
1918 - 1925	Miss Milligan became Mrs Wallace Williamson
1925 - 1930	Miss Elizabeth Robertson Durham became Mrs Ian Bowhill
1930 - 1960	Miss Marjory Druitt
1960 - 1963	Mrs Angela McIntosh who was Mrs Rome's daughter
1963 - 1965	Miss Marjory Druitt
1965 -1968	Mrs Jean Anderson was Miss Jean Donald
1968 - 1971	Mrs Marjorie Draper was Thomas then Peel
1971 - 1982	Miss Marjory Sharpe
1982 -1989	Mrs Anne Sime
1989 - 1992	Mrs Elise Guy
1992 - 1997	Mrs Judy Cuthbertson
1997 - 2003	Mrs Vickie Sandeman
2003 -	Mrs Anne McIntosh

Treasurers of Gullane Ladies' Golf Club

1905 - 1911	Mrs R. M. Watson	1976 - 1980	Mrs Lyn Inglis
1911 - 1921	Mr R.M. Watson	1980 - 1984	Mrs Betty Hunter
1921 - 1923	Mr F. Marshall	1984 - 1993	Mrs Pat Fraser
1923 - 1931	Miss May Lennox	1993 - 1997	Mrs Sally Dunlop
1931 - 1933	Miss Ada Lawrie	1997 - 2001	Mrs Shona Low
1933 - 1976	Miss Marjorie Druitt	2001 -	Mrs Elizabeth Burnet

Handicap Managers (until 1965; not necessarily members of GLGC) and Handicap Secretaries of Gullane Ladies Golf Club

1921 - 1952	Mrs Wallace Williamson	1980- 1982	Mrs Anne Sime
1952 - 1957	Mrs Scott Davidson	1982 -1989	Mrs Barbara McIntosh
1960 - 1965	Miss Donaldson	1989- 1997	Mrs Maureen Woodward
1965 - 1967	Mrs Ian Bowhill	1997- 2001	Mrs Joanne Watt
1967- 1980	Mrs Marjorie Draper	2001-	Mrs Hazel Saunders

APPENDIX 4

GULLANE LADIES' GOLF CLUB CHAMPIONS

Date	Winner
1947	Mrs E.C. Beddows
1948	Miss J. Donald
1949	Miss J. Donald
1950	Mrs R.T. Peel
1951	Mrs R.T. Peel
1952	Miss J. Donald
1953	Miss A.H. Boyd
1954	Mrs R.T. Peel
1955	Mrs T. Woodcock
1956	Mrs R.T. Peel
1957	Mrs T. Woodcock
1958	Mrs E.C. Beddows
1959	Miss M. Fowler
1960	Dr R. Donaldson
1961	Miss M.A. Fowler
1962	Miss M.A. Fowler
1963	Miss M.A. Fowler
1964	Miss M.A. Fowler
1965	Miss M.A. Fowler
1966	Dr R. Donaldson
1967	Miss C. J. Lugton
1968	Miss M Norval
1969	Mrs A.J.R. Ferguson
1970	Mrs A.J.R. Ferguson
1971	Miss C. J. Lugton
1972	Miss C. J. Lugton
1972	Miss L Hope
1973	Miss C. J. Lugton
1974	Miss C. J. Lugton
1975	Miss C. J. Lugton
1976	Miss L.A. Hope
1977	Mrs A.J.R. Ferguson
1978	Miss L.A. Hope
1979	Mrs A.J.R. Ferguso n
1980	Mrs A.J.R. Ferguson
1981	Mrs D.J.H. McIntosh
1982	Miss C. J. Lugton
1983	Mrs D.J.H. McIntosh
1984	Mrs A.J.R. Ferguson
1985	Mrs A.J.R. Ferguson
1986	Miss F.C. Anderson
1987	Miss C. Lambert
1988	Miss C. Lambert
1989	Miss C. Lambert
1990	Miss F.C. Anderson
1991	Miss F.C. Anderson
1992	Miss C. Lambert
1993	Miss F.C. Anderson
1994	Mrs L. Roxburgh
1995	Mrs L. Roxburgh
1996	Mrs L. Roxburgh
1997	Mrs L. Roxburgh
1998	Miss L. Nicholson
1999	Mrs J. Smith
2000	Mrs D.J.H. McIntosh
2001	Ms Shonagh McEwan
2002	Ms L. Anderson

APPENDIX 5

WINNERS OVER THE YEARS

All members of GLGC, past and present, who have won national or major titles are detailed below. Even when they have not been a member at the time or have entered from another club, their achievement has still been recognised.

Winners of the British Ladies' Championship

1934 Mrs A.M. Holm
1938 Mrs A.M. Holm
1952 Miss Moira Paterson
1993 Miss Catriona Lambert

Winners of the Scottish Ladies' Championship

1920 Mrs J.B. Watson (Charlotte Beddows)
1921 Mrs J.B. Watson
1922 Mrs J.B. Watson
1923 Mrs W.H. Nicholson
1925 Mrs H.J. Percy
1926 Miss M.J. Wood
1929 Mrs J.B. Watson
1930 Mrs A.M. Holm (Helen Holm)
1932 Mrs A.M. Holm
1933 Miss M.J. Couper
1935 Miss M.M. Robertson Durham
1936 Miss Doris Park
1937 Mrs A.M.Holm
1947 Miss J. Donald (Jean Anderson)
1948 Mrs A.M. Holm
1949 Miss J. Donald
1950 Mrs A.M. Holm
1952 Miss J. Donald

1954 Mrs R.T. Peel (Marjory Draper)
1969 Mrs J. Anderson (Jean Donald)
1975 Miss Lesley Hope
1977 Miss C.J. Lugton
1987 Miss F. Anderson
1991 Miss C. Lambert
1993 Miss C. Lambert
1994 Miss C. Lambert
1999 Miss Jayne Smith

Winners of English Ladies' Championship

1960 Miss M. Nichol
1969 Miss B. Dixon

Winners of East of Scotland Championship

1947 Miss J. Donald
1948 Miss J. Donald
1949 Miss J. Donald
1951 Mrs R.T. Peel
1952 Mrs R.T. Peel
1953 Miss J. Donald
1954 Mrs R.T. Peel
1955 Mrs R.T. Peel
1956 Mrs R.T. Peel
1957 Mrs R.T. Peel
1959 Miss M. Fowler
1960 Miss M. Fowler
1961 Mrs M. Draper (Peel)

1962	Miss M. Fowler
1974	Miss C. Lugton
1975	Mrs A. Ferguson (Fowler)
1977	Miss L. Hope
1978	Miss L. Hope
1984	Miss L Hope
1988	Miss J. Ford
1989	Miss C. Lambert
1992	Miss J. Ford
1995	Miss L. Nicholson

Winners of East Lothian Championship

1934	Miss M J Couper	1963	Miss M Fowler
1935	Miss M J Couper	1964	Miss M Fowler
1936	Miss M M Robertson Durham	1965	Miss C Lugton
1937	Mrs I Bowhill	1966	Miss M Fowler
1938	Miss M J Couper	1967	Miss M Fowler
1948	Miss J Donald	1968	Miss C Lugton
1949	Miss J Donald	1969	Mrs M Ferguson (Fowler)
1950	Mrs R T Peel	1970	Miss C Lugton
1951	Miss J Donald	1971	Miss C Lugton
1952	Miss J Donald	1972	Miss C Lugton
1953	Miss J Donald	1973	Miss C Lugton
1957	Miss M Fowler	1974	Mrs M Ferguson
1958	Miss M Fowler	1975	Mrs B McIntosh
1959	Miss M Fowler	1976	Miss C Lugton
1960	Miss M Fowler	1977	Miss C Lugton
1961	Miss M Fowler	1980	Miss C Lugton
1962	Miss M Fowler	1981	Mrs M Ferguson

1983 Mrs M Thomson
1984 Mrs M Ferguson
1985 Mrs M Ferguson
1986 Miss P Lees
1987 Miss J Ford
1988 Miss C Lugton
1989 Miss C Lugton
1990 Miss C Lambert
1992 Mrs C Matthew (Lambert)
2003 Mrs J Smith (Ford)

Winning teams over the years

Eglinton Quaich

The Scottish Ladies' Golf Association hold the Eglinton Quaich competition annually. Originally it was a preliminary to the actual competition; now it is part of the qualifying rounds for the knock out competition. This contest is, in effect, the Ladies' Team Championship of Scotland. Originally it was played for on an aggregate basis, each team having four players, the scratch aggregate counting for the Quaich, and the net aggregate for the Grainger Cup. The teams nowadays consist of two players.

The winning teams were:
1908 Miss L Lugton, Miss Alloway, Miss M Cairns, Miss Emma McKenzie
1924 Miss M Wood, Miss D Park, Miss M Thomas, Miss J Brown
1925 Miss M Wood, Miss D Park, Miss M Thomas, Mrs Wallace Williamson
1928 Miss M Wood, Miss D Park, Mrs H Percy, Miss M Couper
1929 Miss D Park, Mrs H Percy, Miss M Couper, Mrs Wallace Williamson
1930 Miss D Park, Mrs H Percy, Miss Robertson Durham, Miss M M Robertson Durham
1934 Miss D Park, Mrs R Peel(nee Thomas), Mrs J Duncan(nee Wood), Miss C Park

1935 Miss D Park, Miss M Couper, Miss M Robertson Durham, Mrs Wallace Williamson
1939 Miss M Couper, Mrs J Duncan, Miss Robertson Durham, Miss C Park
1947 Miss D Park, Miss C Park, Miss J Donald, Mrs E C Beddows
1948 Miss C Park, Miss J Donald, Mrs E C Beddows, Miss M Paterson
1949 Miss J Donald, Mrs R T Peel, Miss M Paterson, Miss M Thompson
1950 Miss J Donald, Mrs R Peel, Miss M Paterson, Mrs Wm Ritchie(nee Park)
1951 Miss J Donald, Mrs R Peel, Miss M Paterson, Mrs Wm Ritchie
1952 Miss J Donald, Mrs R Peel, Miss M Paterson, Mrs Wm Ritchie
1955 Mrs R Peel, Mrs W Ritchie, Mrs T Woodcock, Mrs J D McIntosh
1959 Mrs R Peel, Mrs W Ritchie, Miss M Fowler, Miss E Philip
1979 Miss L Hope, Miss C Lugton
1986 Miss L Hope, Mrs M Ferguson (nee Fowler)

Grainger Cup
Lowest nett team aggregate

1934 Mrs Birkbeck, Mrs Percy, Mrs Wallace Williamson, Miss Robertson Durham
1937 Miss D Park, Miss Robertson Durham, Mrs I Bowhill, Miss C Park
1952 Mrs H Rogers, Mrs J Groom, Mrs Woodcock, Mrs Mackie
1953 Miss L Dunbar, Mrs Cuthbertson, Mrs Oppenheim, Mrs J Henderson
1962 Mrs J Wishart, Mrs C Draper, Miss M Fowler, Miss E Philip
1963 Miss M Fowler, Mrs G H Hay, Miss C Corstorphine, Miss C Lugton
1964 Miss M Fowler, Mrs M Ritchie, Mrs G H Hay, Miss C Lugton
1967 Mrs J Milton, Mrs G Gordon, Mrs A L McLure, Mrs J R Ness
1969 Miss F Miller, Mrs P Jack, Mrs J C Milton, Mrs A H Campbell
1976 Miss L Hope, Mrs A Ferguson

APPENDIX 6

LADIES' CHAMPIONSHIPS HELD AT GULLANE

British Ladies' Amateur Championship	1897, 1947, 1970, 2004
Scottish Ladies' Amateur Championship	1908, 1925, 1931, 1952, 1964, 1979, 1994
British Ladies' Amateur Stroke Play Championship	1993
Ladies' Home Internationals	1947, 1960, 1984, 1990
British Girls Amateur Championship	1951, 1963
Scottish Girls Amateur Championship	1959
Scottish Ladies County Finals	1959, 1962, 1999
East of Scotland Ladies' Championship	1935, 1947, 1951, 1953, 1954, 1991
Vets Jamboree	1984, 1996

APPENDIX 7

S.L.G.A. SONG

Song sung in 1984 at the Scottish Ladies' Championship dinner to the tune of "We belong to Glasgow".

We belong to Gullane
THE Ladies'Golfing club.
We're jolly exclusive and you'd be out
If you failed to pay your sub.
We're frightfully social, we're lots of fun
As anyone here can see.
The men are complaining that WE'RE entertaining
You gels at this S.L.A.C.

Teams have come to play here
At Gullane by the sea,
Baberton, Cruden Bay, Douglas Park
Kingsknowe and Turnberree.
It's great to be having a tournament,
We're thrilled to be hosting this bash.
We've watched you lot starring and soon we'll be parring
Instead of our usual trash.

What a stack of trophies
Waiting to be won.
There's Grainger's Cup and a Clark Rosebowl
And a quaich from Eglinton.
There's salvers in silver and bowls in gold
Just fill them all up from the tap.
But try to stay sober, a raging hangover
Could well be a handicap.

What a lot of effort
Goes on behind the scenes.
From organisational paperwork
To the chaps who cut the greens.
We'd like to name all of you personally

But there just isn't room in this rhyme.
Mrs Bauer, McCarrol, Anderson, Lackie and Park
Thank you all-and of course Anne Sime.

We hope you've all enjoyed Gullane
Playing round and round.
Practice and qualify, stroke and match
Before a chap is found.
So home to bed early for Finals Day,
It's time for your Ralgex rub.
And when you get home on the Saturday you will say
Gullane's a fine wee club!

Elaine Carnie Captain 1999 - 2000

INDEX